LOVE HIM
EVER MORE

"Fr. Joe Laramie has provided us with a spiritual guide that is both practical and sublime."

Mark E. Thibodeaux, SJ
Author of *Ascending with Ignatius*

"Fr. Joe Laramie helps the busy, modern reader learn to love and serve Jesus more with *Love Him Ever More*. Jesus has a beating heart, just like ours. Fr. Laramie invites us to take time to pray about how much that heart loves us—and the world—so that we can join our lives to his mission."

Zac Davis
Cohost of the *Jesuitical* podcast

"Every year a book comes along that revitalizes what it means to be in relationship with the Lord. *Love Him Ever More* brilliantly achieves this by accompanying us on a journey towards the Lord with humor and gentleness. Fr. Joe Laramie has an amazing way of familiarizing you with the Sacred Heart through personal anecdotes and inviting reflection questions. He is a gift to the Church and *Love Him Ever More* is a gift to God's people!"

Chenele Shaw
Host of the *Ave Spotlight* podcast

"I found *Love Him Ever More* to be engaging, spiritually impactful, and heartwarming. I highly recommend this self-guided retreat by Fr. Joe Laramie."

Emily Jaminet
Author of *Secrets of the Sacred Heart*

LOVE HIM EVER MORE

A 9-DAY PERSONAL RETREAT
with the SACRED HEART *of* JESUS

Based on the *Spiritual Exercises* of St. Ignatius Loyola

FR. JOE LARAMIE, SJ

AVE MARIA PRESS AVE Notre Dame, Indiana

Nihil Obstat:	Reverend Thomas L. Knoebel, PhD
	February 1, 2022
Imprimatur:	Very Reverend Jerome Listecki, Archbishop of Milwaukee
	February 28, 2022
Imprimi Potest:	Very Reverend Thomas P. Greene, SJ, Provincial
	USA Central and Southern Province of the Society of Jesus

All excerpts from St. Ignatius's *Spiritual Exercises* are cited with *SE* and a number. This is the paragraph number, which is consistent across editions and translations. Excerpts from the translation by George E. Ganss, S.J., Chestnut Hill, MA: Institute of Jesuit Sources, 1992. Used with permission from the Institute for Advanced Jesuit Studies, Boston College.

Section from "Day 3: Broken Hearts," adapted from author's essay, "A Deadly Crash on the Feast of the Assumption," *America*, August 2019, americamagazine.org/faith/2019/08/15/deadly-crash-feast-assumption; reprinted with permission of America Press, Inc., 2022. All rights reserved.

Unless noted otherwise, scripture texts in this work are taken from the *New American Bible, revised edition* © 2010, 1991, 1986, 1970 Confraternity of Christian Doctrine, Washington, DC, and are used by permission of the copyright owner. All rights reserved. No part of the *New American Bible* may be reproduced in any form without permission in writing from the copyright owner.

Frontispiece Photo "A Statue of the Sacred Heart of Jesus" © MART PRODUCTION on Pexels.com.

Founded in 1865, Ave Maria Press is a ministry of the United States Province of Holy Cross.

www.avemariapress.com

Paperback: ISBN-13 978-1-64680-154-1

E-book: ISBN-13 978-1-64680-155-8

Cover image © BenedictaBoutique, benedictaboutique.etsy.com.

Cover and text design by Brianna Dombo.

Printed and bound in the United States of America.

Library of Congress Cataloging-in-Publication Data is available.

CONTENTS

ACKNOWLEDGMENTS

Whenever I prepare a homily, I ask Christ, "What do you want me to say to your people?" Without fail, the message is, "Tell them I love them." That is also the message of this book: Jesus telling you and showing you how he loves you.

I'm grateful to many faithful people who helped me with this book. First, I want to thank Fr. Frederic Fornos, SJ, international director of the Pope's Worldwide Prayer Network (Apostleship of Prayer). He developed the nine steps of The Way of the Heart several years ago and promoted it in a variety of formats and languages: online, with an app and e-book, and more.[1] Inspired by his work, I'm honored to share this spiritual pathway in English in North America.

A very big thanks to Catherine Owers and Ave Maria Press. Thanks for giving me a chance with my first book, *Abide in the Heart of Christ*, and for giving me another opportunity with a second book. To quote the popular musical *Hamilton*, "I'm not throwing away my shot!" With both books, Catherine helped me to unpack Jesuit vocabulary and the Sacred Heart devotion to make these topics accessible to a wide audience. Both books are clearer and more readable because of her sharp mind, faithful heart, and careful editing.

Warm gratitude to the staff of PWPN North America. Our team is "young, scrappy, and hungry" like Alexander Hamilton—and the first apostles. I'll highlight Fr. Edmund Lo, SJ (PWPN Canada), Katie Breitenbach, Danny Chekal, Noah Smith, and Emily Davenport: they read drafts and offered quality feedback. Thanks to my superiors for supporting me.

Thanks to my family, Jesuit buddies, and lay friends for listening to me talk about this book over beer, coffee, and/or meals over the last two years. Thanks for listening, sharing, and laughing.

Love and gratitude to three popes who have guided my vocation: St. John Paul II, Benedict XVI, and Francis. I entered the Jesuits under the first, was ordained under the second, and write this book under the third. St. John Paul II, the zealous shepherd, prays for us from heaven. The wise shepherd, Benedict XVI, prays for us as pope emeritus. Francis, the merciful shepherd, leads the Church on earth. Inspired by the Good Shepherd, each man has challenged me, taught me, and inspired me with his words, prayers, and actions. As director of the Pope's Worldwide Prayer Network in the United States, I say, "*Viva el Papa!*"

Finally, thanks to all those who read my first book and all who are reading this one. Thank you for taking time for prayer and reflection. You are trusting me to assist you. I don't take this for granted. I'm praying for you. Please pray for me.

INTRODUCTION

Whoever wishes to come with me must labor
with me, so that through following me in the
pain, he or she may follow me also in the
glory.
—*Spiritual Exercises*,[1] 95

Put your hand on your heart. Feel your heartbeat. Perhaps your heart is beating slowly and peacefully. Maybe you are sitting in your favorite chair, in a quiet moment at the end of the day. Or maybe your heart is beating fast. You're rushing back from work, school, or some errands. Note the emotions underneath your heartbeat. This may be a sense of quiet joy and hope in this time of reflection; today was a good day and you're feeling grateful. Or maybe there is a tug of anxiety on your heart as you recall an unpleasant conversation with a colleague or think about a sick relative.

In the gospels, we see Jesus experiencing the whole range of human emotions: joy, sorrow, loneliness, and even anger. He invites us to unite our emotions and our experiences with his Sacred Heart.

Your heart is beating right now. So is his.

Your heart is made for love.

Your heart is made for relationship with Christ and with others.

He became man for us and has a body and a heart to be in closer communion with us.

His heart beats with love for the Father and for each of us.

Christ shaped your heart in the image and likeness of his heart.

Before we begin our retreat together, let's look at a few key topics and terms.

WHAT DOES IT MEAN TO "LOVE HIM EVER MORE"?

To "love him ever more" is a pathway of uniting our hearts with the heart of Jesus for the salvation of all hearts. In his heart we can transform the world, one heart at a time, starting with our hearts. This book is a nine-day retreat. As Jesus calls us to deeper communion, he plunges us into his mission of compassion in the world around us. This journey continues in the spirit of my first book, *Abide in the Heart of Christ: A 10-Day Personal Retreat with St. Ignatius Loyola based on the* Spiritual Exercises (Ave Maria Press, 2019). In my first book, I focused on renewing, healing, and strengthening our hearts by abiding in the heart of Christ. If you read the first book, it will help you with the context and spirit of St. Ignatius. If you haven't read it, that's okay—I'll go over the basics, and we'll continue our spiritual journey.

In *Love Him Ever More*, the second book, we briefly review where we've traveled and then pick up where we left off, by sharing in the mission of Jesus: the salvation of all hearts. *Love Him Ever More* is a journey of prayer to renew and spread the Sacred Heart devotion in the world today. In Christ, our hearts are united in a mission of compassion for the needs of the Church and the world.

HOW IS EACH DAY ORGANIZED?

We start with the title, which is the topic we'll focus on. Then I give a brief quote from St. Ignatius related to the topic. Next, I offer a brief "grace" to pray for during this day. I'll then share a personal story to illustrate. After that, I connect the topic to the *Spiritual Exercises* of St. Ignatius. We'll then move into a contemplative prayer experience; here we often use our imagination and five senses, and we'll often engage Jesus in a specific gospel passage—with a special focus on his Sacred Heart. We conclude each day with a few questions and "exercises" (a format similar to my first book). Finally, we close with a short prayer. In our retreat, we're not primarily seeking information but formation of our hearts according to the heart of Jesus.

WHAT ARE THE NINE DAYS
OF *LOVE HIM EVER MORE?*

Before you travel somewhere, you *consider* the route you'll take to get there. In this retreat, I'll often use the image of "journey" in my examples and stories. A pathway implies movement and traveling with Jesus. The nine days of *Love Him Ever More* are divided into three parts: "My Heart," "His Heart," and "All Hearts."

Days 1 through 3 look at our own hearts. We reflect on our lives, our faith, and our specific context in the world. Our hearts are made by a loving God; he desires to be in relationship with each one of us. As we look at our own heart, we thank the Lord for the many blessings he has given us. Our hearts are wounded by sin. We need healing, grace, and mercy. Here we will see connections to themes in my first book, *Abide in the Heart of Christ*. I hope to deepen and expand these themes in *Love Him Ever More*.

Days 4 through 6 focus on the heart of Jesus and his call for us. We'll consider his Incarnation, calling us as friends and disciples, and his promise to be with us always. We experience his abiding presence concretely in the Church and in the Eucharist.

In days 7 through 9, we consider his call to join him on mission. We can offer ourselves to him each day with the Daily Offering Prayer (day 7). For some, this may mean a more devoted commitment to family life. For others, it could be greater service in one's parish or even a heroic call to missionary service. In *Evangelii Gaudium (The Joy of the Gospel)*, Pope Francis says that "we are all missionary disciples. . . . Throughout the world, let us be 'permanently in a state of mission'" (119, 25). This means in our homes and neighborhoods, in our hearts, and in faraway lands. Increasingly we seek to see the world through the eyes of Jesus, to offer our hearts to him, and to join him in his mission of redemption. With him, in the Church, we seek to touch the hearts of others through prayer and action.

WHO IS THIS BOOK FOR?

You. You can use it alone, with a friend, or in a group. You don't need a master's degree in theology. All you need is an open mind, an open heart, and a desire to grow closer to Christ.

If you do this retreat with others, I encourage you to first take some time in personal prayer, reflection, and journaling. Then you can share some insights and graces with a friend.

WHAT IS IGNATIAN SPIRITUALITY?

St. Ignatius Loyola uses several methods of prayer in the *Spiritual Exercises*. Together, these methods are often called Ignatian spirituality. All these methods were used by other saints and Christian writers; however, Ignatius applies them with freshness and power. I drew on some of these methods in my first book, *Abide in the Heart of Christ*. One method is the Examen, which involves looking back on our experience in the light of God's grace. For example, I may want to look over this past week with gratitude, thanking God for the many gifts I have received. Or I may need to look over my life and clearly see my own sins; perhaps I notice patterns of sin in my life. I can ask God to help me make positive changes in the future. Another method is called *lectio divina*. There, we slowly and prayerfully read through a prayer or Bible passage. Word by word, we ask God how he is speaking to us in these lines. For example, in psalm 23, "The LORD is my shepherd." I may see these first few words and pray, "Lord, I see how you are my shepherd. You have guided and protected me in these moments of my life . . ." Slowly I move to the next line of the psalm, "there is nothing I lack." Here I may consider, "Lord, you do give me what I need: family, friends, food, and faith. Sometimes I've struggled, but you've never let me down . . ." In this book, we'll especially use a method of prayer called Ignatian contemplation.

WHAT IS IGNATIAN CONTEMPLATION?

Ignatian contemplation, sometimes called "imaginative prayer," is one of several ways to read scripture.

One way to approach scripture is a literal/historical reading. In this way, we simply read a particular book or passage of the Bible to get a basic understanding of what is happening—the main story line for certain key characters such as Moses, David, and so forth. Another way to approach scripture is with a moral/ethical method. Here, we're looking for the moral of the story and what it means for each of us: How am I living these teachings? How am I falling short? Where do I need God's help in a special way? This can be fruitful with passages such as the Ten Commandments or the Beatitudes.

A deeper way to read scripture is the contemplative method outlined by St. Ignatius, which builds on the literal/historical and moral/ethical methods and helps draw us into closer relationship with Jesus. We use our imaginations and our five senses—seeing, hearing, tasting, touching, and smelling—to engage Jesus, Mary, and the disciples in the gospels at a personal level.

Let's briefly consider the calming of the storm at sea in Matthew 14. The disciples are in the boat. Jesus is praying on the mountain. The wind and waves rise, and the boat is "tossed about" (Mt 14:24). Smell the smells with the disciples. The cold fresh rain splatters down into the fishy aroma of an old boat and the heavy wet clothing of twelve men. We may recall a time we were in a boat or near a large body of water, the boat sloshing and shifting beneath us as it rides over the waves. The darkness is everywhere, shattered only by the flash of lightning.

Focus now on these disciples; see their strain as they pull on the oars. Wrinkles of stress, fear, and exhaustion mark their sunburned foreheads. Just when things can't get worse, they see a figure approaching. "It is a ghost!" they cry out. Jesus speaks to them, "Take courage, it is I; do not be afraid" (Mt 14:26–27). Hear his words spoken firmly and calmly as he stands on the rolling waves. We use this method to engage Jesus and the apostles in a "spiritual conversation"—speaking and listening "heart to heart," or as St. Ignatius describes, "the way one friend speaks to another" (*SE*, 54). We each consider, "How do I feel as I look at the disciples? When I look at Jesus and hear his words? What am I afraid of? What storms does he want to calm in my heart?"

In a way, all Christian artists use this method of prayer. As Michelangelo reflected on the *Pietà*, he used his imagination to prayerfully consider how Mary would look and feel when she saw her son taken down from the cross after his Crucifixion. Michelangelo's sculpture masterfully captures this moment; we, too, feel drawn into her experience as we contemplate this mother's sorrow.

We often find that by contemplatively revisiting and repeating a topic in prayer, we can continue to strengthen and grow in the graces that Christ offers to us. Each time we do this, the prayer will be slightly different, of course; perhaps our own disposition has changed, or we notice something special in the words or actions of Jesus. St. Ignatius calls this "savoring" or "relishing" the graces. We find this in our own daily lives as well. A couple may go back to a favorite restaurant again and again; they know and love the place, have many fond memories of their meals and conversations there, and their experience is always fresh and alive with each new visit. That's what can happen in prayer, too.

Sometimes people get nervous about using their imagination to pray with the gospels. They wonder, "What if I'm just making it up? How do I know if I'm doing it right?" Certainly, if we notice that our prayer is drifting out of Church teaching, then we want to re-center it. If St. Peter tells me that my sins *can't* be forgiven, then I know I'm off track. If I get confused,

I go back to the text. What is happening? Who is there? What is being said? This kind of prayer requires patience and trust. Sometimes little children are better at it than adults!

HOW SHOULD I USE THIS BOOK?

You may choose to do this retreat over nine consecutive days. You may want to begin or end your retreat on a first Friday of the month since this day is especially devoted to the Sacred Heart of Jesus. Or you could do this retreat over nine weeks—perhaps setting aside time each Sunday for prayer and reflection. You can do this retreat alone, with a spouse or friend, or in a small group. If you do this retreat with others, you should first take some time in quiet prayer alone and then share and discuss some of the graces with others.

DO I NEED ANY OTHER
SUPPLIES FOR THIS RETREAT?

All you need for this retreat is an open mind, an open heart, a Bible, a pen, and a journal or notebook. In particular, you can use your journal when you are reflecting on the questions at the end of each chapter. A journal is like a net that helps you to catch the graces that God offers to you in prayer and reflection. Just jotting down a few words and images can be helpful. Also, this allows you to go back and revisit these graces later. I'll reflect on several gospel passages during this retreat. I invite you to read and pray with these passages on your own, too. If you are a baptized Christian, then this is your book and your story. I hope my insights are helpful, and you can go deeper by talking to Christ about these words in person. If you prefer to take notes on a computer or phone, that is fine, too. Be sure to find a good "prayer spot" for this—maybe your favorite chair, a nearby chapel or park, or even your car!

HOW LONG WILL THIS TAKE?

You will need twenty to thirty minutes to read each chapter ("day"), and then another twenty to thirty minutes for prayer and reflection. If you wish, the reading and prayer could take place within a "holy hour" each day. *Love Him Ever More* is a nine-step retreat. In this sense it is a kind of novena (a nine-day prayer in which you ask God for a particular grace or blessing).

WHAT GRACES WILL I RECEIVE IN THIS RETREAT?

St. Ignatius Loyola summarizes the grace that we seek: "To know Jesus more, love him more, and serve him more" (see *SE*, 104). If you already know, love, and serve Jesus in some ways, this retreat will deepen your relationship with him. If you feel like a spiritual beginner or you are a spiritual seeker looking for meaning and direction in life, I explain and unpack the key concepts so that everyone can understand and reflect on them. For all of us, *Love Him Ever More* can guide us to deeper communion with Christ. A closer encounter with him renews us, rejuvenates our hearts, and channels our energy to serve him more fully. After encountering the risen Jesus on the road to Emmaus, the two disciples cry out, "Were not our hearts burning [within us] while he spoke to us on the way?" (Lk 24:32). This is our prayer: that the Sacred Heart of Jesus may set our hearts on fire.

WHAT IS THE SACRED HEART?

The Sacred Heart is an ancient Christian devotion to the heart of Jesus. He has a living beating heart right now. His heart pours out love and grace for you, me, and all people. Devotion to his Sacred Heart began when Mother Mary felt his tiny heart beating beneath her heart as he was formed in her womb more than two thousand years ago. Many saints, mystics, and theologians have prayed and spoken about his Sacred Heart through the centuries—including St. Augustine, St. Gertrude, and St. Margaret Mary Alacoque. The Sacred Heart helps us to focus on the love of Jesus as well as his humanity. He has a heart, and we do, too. He loves us, and we want to love him ever more.

WHAT IS THE POPE'S WORLDWIDE PRAYER NETWORK (APOSTLESHIP OF PRAYER)?

This 175-year-old Jesuit ministry promotes a life of prayer for all people. Daily, we offer our hearts to the heart of Jesus for the salvation of all hearts. It was begun in France in 1844 by a group of young Jesuits who wanted to serve in the missions of

North America, Asia, and beyond. Their superior called them to be "Apostles of Prayer" by offering their hearts to Christ. This practice gradually spread to lay students, surrounding French villages, Europe, and the United States. I'm honored to continue this beautiful ministry in the twenty-first century. In particular, we pray for the monthly intentions of the Holy Father, Pope Francis—our first Jesuit pope! The original name of the organization was the Apostleship of Prayer. We use this name along with our new name, the Pope's Worldwide Prayer Network. The new name emphasizes the universal nature of our group and our special relationship with the Holy Father.

> Pray "to know him more, love him more,
> and serve him more" (see *SE*, 104).

Questions and Exercises

Note: as you read these questions, jot down a few words and phrases in your journal or notebook. Even a few images or phrases can be helpful. Also, you can return to these reflections later to continue and deepen your prayer.

What is one specific grace you are hoping to receive from this retreat? Perhaps peace, a sense of direction, or healing?

Ask the Lord what graces he wants to give you during this retreat. These may be the same as the ones you seek—or perhaps something different, or even bigger than you dared to ask!

You may want to call upon a saint to walk with you during this retreat. This might be St. Ignatius, Mother Mary, the angel Gabriel, or another patron. Take a moment to ask this person to pray for you and journey with you.

At the beginning of this retreat, take a moment in prayer to offer your heart to Christ. He is your true spiritual director and guide on this spiritual journey. You may want to use the Daily Offering prayer (day 7) or the Suscipe (day 9).

LITANY OF THE SACRED HEART

Pray the opening lines of the Litany of the Sacred Heart. (The prayer appears in its entirety in the appendix.)

Heart of Jesus, Son of the Eternal Father: Have mercy on us.

Heart of Jesus, formed in the womb of the Virgin Mother by the Holy Spirit: Have mercy on us.

Heart of Jesus, united substantially with the word of God: Have mercy on us.

PART I

MY HEART:

REFLECTION, GRATITUDE, HEALING

HE LOVES US FIRST

Consider how all good things and gifts
descend from above . . . justice, goodness,
piety, mercy and so forth—just as the rays
come down from the sun, or the rains from
their source.
—*Spiritual Exercises*, 237

I don't remember my nine months in the womb. I imagine I loved it there. Those first nine months were a "school of the heart": my heart was formed; I was loved by God and by my family. I was in a place of peace, rest, warmth, and safety. Hearing my mom's gentle hum as she went about her day—running errands, doing yard work, and preparing my room. My little heart, beating underneath my mom's heart; a little duet of life and love. The murmur of kind words and blessings from relatives at family gatherings. "You're having a boy! I'm so happy for you! When's he due?" My birth was a big shock for me, I'm sure—the hospital's bright lights, cold air; a doctor in a white coat grabbing me, cleaning me, weighing and measuring me. This was followed by more comforting moments: being wrapped in blankets, kissed by Mom, and held by Dad. Weeks later I'd be brought to church for Baptism at my home parish, Sacred Heart Church, a soaring gothic structure outside St. Louis built by German immigrants in the late 1800s. Fr. Jack Schuler baptized me. He is my dad's cousin; he was in his mid-twenties then, dressed in white vestments, recently ordained. While my grandparents and godparents sang and prayed, Fr. Jack poured water over me, baptizing, "Joseph William, I baptize you in the name of the Father, and of the Son, and of the Holy Spirit." With holy oil, he traced the Cross on my forehead and over my heart, sealing me with the grace of Holy Spirit.

In John's gospel, we see the heart of Jesus pierced by the soldier's lance as he hangs on the cross, and out pours blood and water. The water is an image of Baptism, and his blood is poured out in the Eucharist at every Mass. Truly the sacraments of the Church flow from his Sacred Heart. In the church of the Sacred Heart, my tiny heart was drawn into the love of his mighty heart.

This is the mystery of Christian life. We are made in love by a loving God. "God is love," as St. John tells us (1 Jn 4:8). A few lines later, he writes, "He first loved us" (1 Jn 4:19). My parents, family, and parish were tangible signs of this love. I did not earn this love nor even ask for it. This gift of love was simply given to me in love.

As a priest, I've worked with young couples preparing for Baptism. Together they hope, pray, wait, and love—entrusting their child to Christ through the Church even before seeing the child's face. A mother gently places her hand on her tummy, feeling the movements of her unborn child, singing and humming even before she sees the child's face. The father also shares in this loving gesture, putting his hand on his wife's hand, smiling, gently patting, and saying, "Love you, baby. We'll see you in a few weeks." They talk to and pray for their child; they choose a name. Their love for their child is an image of God's love for the child. This love is unconditional and joyful. God's love is eternal and infinite. While his love is always greater than human love, like these parents, his "love is patient, [his] love is kind. It is not jealous. . . . [His] love never fails" (1 Cor 13:4, 8).

Looking at this couple, I imagine what my own parents must have thought and felt. As Christians, we ask to live in this sense of wonder. God loves us. God creates us in love. God places us in a family and in the Church in great love. God is love.

OVERVIEW OF THE DAY FROM IGNATIUS: LOVE IS THE BEGINNING

In the *Spiritual Exercises*, St. Ignatius writes, "I will see and consider the three Divine Persons, seated, so to speak, on the royal canopied throne of their Divine Majesty. They are gazing on the whole face and circuit of the earth; and they see all the peoples" (*SE*, 106). As we begin this journey with the heart of Jesus, let's consider this truth: *in the beginning there was love.* We hear these words echoed in three places in the Bible. The book of Genesis opens, "In the beginning, when God created the heavens and the earth" (1:1). We see this phrase again at the start of John's gospel: "In the beginning was the Word" (1:1). And, third, "God is love" (1 Jn 4:8). God was there when the world began. God existed even before the world was created. God is spirit, God is eternal and infinite, and God is love. God made us, loves us, and sees us. We are made by God and placed in a family. We are made for relationship with God and with others. We are created in love. We are created for love.

> "Ponder with deep affection how much
> God our Lord has done for me, and
> how much he has given me of what he
> possesses" (*SE*, 234).

CONTEMPLATION:
EXPERIENCING GOD'S LOVE

We will start in the glory of heaven, beholding the eternal Trinity. John's gospel begins at the beginning, before time began:

> In the beginning was the Word,
> and the Word was with God,
> and the Word was God.
> He was in the beginning with God.
> All things came to be through him,
> and without him nothing came to be.
> What came to be through him was life,
> and this life was the light of the human race;

> the light shines in the darkness,
> and the darkness has not overcome it. (Jn
> 1:1–5)

Let's use our imagination to reflect on this scene. We first use the sense of sight as we ask to see and consider the blessed Trinity in the glory of heaven. Here we may recall scenes from Christian art to help us see God. In the Sistine Chapel, Michelangelo portrays God the Father as a strong, wise man, with a purple robe and flowing beard. The Holy Spirit is sometimes seen as a dove, a flame, or a wise man like God the Father.

As we profess in the Nicene Creed, we believe in "God from God, Light from Light, true God from true God." God is Father, Son, and Spirit. God is a family, a community, a relationship. God is a Trinity of Divine Persons. Some artists portray the Trinity as three divine kings lovingly presiding over creation. Others paint this as an image of glory and light. Let us also use our sense of hearing. Some saints hear the Trinity as a symphony of three notes sung in perfect harmony. What might the Trinity say to one another? St. Ignatius invites us to "hear what the Divine Persons are saying." We hear words between Jesus and the Father in the gospels: "This is my beloved Son, with whom I am well pleased," says the Father (Mt 3:17). Jesus says, "Now glorify me, Father, with you, with the glory that I had with you before the world began" (Jn 17:5). Jesus proclaims, "I am in the Father and the Father is in me" (Jn 14:11).

St. Ignatius also encourages each of us to "reflect upon myself to draw some profit" (*SE*, 114). We may ask, "How do

I feel as I reflect upon the glory of God? Joyful and hopeful? Overwhelmed and confused?" Maybe our hearts are moved with humility as we consider our own weakness before God's grandeur.

Next, let us look at the beauty of God's creation. "I will consider how all good things and gifts descend from above . . . just as rays come down from the sun, or the rains from their source" (*SE*, 237). God says, "Let there be light, and there was light" (Gn 1:3). "We hold these truths to be self-evident," states the US Constitution, "that all men are created equal." The beauty and goodness of the created world is similarly self-evident: take a walk in a park near your house. Open your eyes to see the sun, the clouds, and the trees. Open your ears to hear the birds chirping, children playing, and dogs barking. Smell the flowers. Feel the soft, wet grass with your hand and the cool wind blowing on your cheek. These are tangible signs of God's goodness. Ponder "how much God our Lord has done for me, and how much he has given me of what he possesses, and consequently how he, the same Lord, desires to give me" (*SE*, 234).

Now consider God creating you. God handcrafted you in great love, from the first moment of your conception. For this part of the contemplation, you may want to find some of your baby pictures in an old photo album. Is there a sonogram or ultrasound image of you? At that visit, the doctor may have placed a stethoscope on your mom's stomach and said, "I can hear the heartbeat. Do you want to listen?" Placing the headset on your mom, she could now hear your tiny heartbeat. God shapes this heart and loves this heart, your heart. In the photos, look at your parents looking at you. Perhaps they were a young couple, and you were their firstborn. Or maybe they were older, and you were a surprise pregnancy! If you were adopted, then consider how your adopted parents felt when they received you. With great trust, your birth mother offered you to adoptive parents who received you with anticipation and gratitude. Similarly, you may want to find photos of your baptism or your baptismal certificate. For many of us, this moment occurred when we were tiny babies, before we were consciously aware of Christ drawing us in to his divine life and love. Through the priest, through the Church, Christ himself baptized us. Using your imagination, you can reflect on the songs that were sung that day, the scent of the candles, the smiles on the faces of your family and friends.

Now look at God looking at you. "I will raise my mind and think how God our Lord is looking at me, and other such thoughts. Then I will make an act of reverence" (*SE*, 75). Reflect how this is the same Divine Trinity I beheld earlier, gazing at the world with wisdom and love. Now, God looks upon me from the first moments of my life. God gazes upon me now and always with great love.

Questions and Exercises

1. What is your favorite image of God? Perhaps Christ the Good Shepherd or the Sacred Heart of Jesus. What draws you to this image? What aspects of God are emphasized:

power, compassion, wisdom? If you have this image in your house, take a few minutes in prayerful reflection before this image. Or you may want to look for one online; consider using it as the "wallpaper" on your phone for the week.

2. Reread the opening lines of the book of Genesis. Imagine that you were there as a witness. We see images of Michelangelo's masterpiece in the Sistine Chapel, portraying the creation of the world. Let your heart be moved with wonder and awe. Jot down a few words describing this scene in your journal.

3. Reflect on God creating you. Look at God looking at you with love in the first moments of your life. Find a few baby pictures of yourself or photos of your baptism. Who was there with you? How do they look? How do they look at you? How do you feel as you ponder this experience?

4. Is there anything you want to say to God in prayer now? Is there anything he wants to say to you?

5. For those who read Abide in the Heart of Christ, go back to your Spiritual Top 10 list. Review these moments and thank God for them. These are moments of special closeness to God. They might include weddings, family vacations, or other experiences (a retreat, time in prayer, etc.).

MY CREATOR AT MY CREATION

Lord, you have searched me and you know me:
you know when I sit and stand;
you understand my thoughts from afar.
You created the moon and the stars,
And in great love you made me in your image and
    likeness.
From the first moments of my life,
As you formed me in my mother's womb,
You shaped my very face
Before my mother could kiss my face.
I praise you, because I am wonderfully made;
Know me, God, and know my heart.

—adapted from Psalm 139

MY HEART IS MADE FOR LOVE

It is characteristic of the evil spirit to cause gnawing anxiety, to sadden, and to set up obstacles. In this way he unsettles these person by false reasons. . . . It is characteristic of the good spirit to stir up courage and strength, consolations, tears, inspirations, and tranquility.
—*Spiritual Exercises*, 315

I was in college, sitting in a small classroom. The room was packed with juniors and seniors: seminarians and seekers, hippies and honor students. Several women sat in the front rows, some of the smartest I've ever met. They were prelaw students who went on to Ivy League graduate schools. I was excited, interested, and intimidated. Through the narrow windows we watched as autumn leaves waved in the winds as the orange sun slid toward the skyline. Every Tuesday and Thursday, 2:00 to 3:15 p.m., we studied modern philosophy, covering the years 1600–1900, with thinkers such as Descartes, Sartre, and Kant. What is true? What isn't? And how do we know? Can we know anything at all?

These were the greatest minds in history tackling the biggest questions. Sometimes they agreed, and often they didn't. Some were Christians, and many weren't. A few seemed to live peaceful lives. Several suffered from mental illness, depression, and alcoholism. I had several friends in the class. We would meet for coffee afterward to go through our notes and prepare for the next paper or test. We talked through existentialism, skepticism, subjectivism, and Descartes's famous quote, "I think, therefore I am."

These topics had crossed my mind, but I hadn't thought about them in depth. I was dating a bit—and considering a call to the priesthood. More immediately, I needed to decide on a major. I was finishing my core classes, and I had enjoyed many of them. What should I focus on? What profession should I prepare for? Journalism? Education? Philosophy?

Life is complicated! I felt like I had a huge buffet spread out before me—steaming platters of my hopes and fears, desires and possibilities, worldviews and philosophies. What should I study? How should I live? What should I do with my life? Which bubbling tray would I find satisfying, nourishing, and fulfilling? Which might be sour and bitter—or worse, sweet at first but ultimately empty or poisonous?

I read the books. I listened to the lectures. I looked around the room. What spoke to my heart? It was the people in the desks around me. Several young Jesuits sat in class next to me, many of them taking classes at Saint Louis University as part of their formation for priesthood. I joined them for study sessions before the big tests. I knew them from retreats and service projects around campus. They were a bit older than me, like big brothers. On occasion they'd invite me over for Mass and dinner. There, I got to see them "in their native habitat"—eating, talking, praying, laughing, washing dishes together. They took their studies seriously. What is the meaning of life? Or rather, who stands at the center of all life and gives it meaning?

I was writing for the school newspaper, and I worked as a DJ for the campus radio station, KSLU. I was involved in retreats and service projects through campus ministry. I remember going to Mass in the school's soaring gothic church. I looked at the crucifix; I saw the priest at the altar; I beheld the Eucharist. Christ gives us himself. He pours out his life in the Incarnation, becomes man for us. He shares his Body and Blood with us in the Eucharist. Most dramatically, he gives his life for us in the Crucifixion. He does all of this for us—for me. What should I do for him? Hold back? Choose the easiest and most lucrative profession? Or profess my faith in him? At every Mass he tells me, "Take this; this is my Body given up for you." As I watched the priest raise the chalice and host at every Mass, I wondered what it would be like to be in those vestments and pray those words. What would it be like to preach a homily? Maybe Christ was calling me to say those words, "Take this, all of you," and to live his offering each day.

At every retreat, every conversation with a Jesuit, every Mass, I felt like Christ was calling me to something deeper, to a closer relationship with him. It was not a demand but an invitation. I could turn it down. I could turn him down. What if I did give my whole life to him? Consistently, the response came in prayer: if I gave myself completely to Christ, then I would be a priest.

OVERVIEW OF THE DAY FROM IGNATIUS: CALLED TO LIVE MY FAITH

As a young man, Ignatius pondered his own path in life. He grew up in a large, wealthy Catholic family in northern Spain. He was well educated, well connected, athletic, and brave. How should he live? What should he do with his gifts? Where would his path lead? He eventually set his sights on a position in the Spanish government. This would be a place of honor for himself and his family while contributing to the glory of Spain and the king. He also saw that he needed to "build his resume" to get this kind of job. In his late twenties, he enlisted in the Spanish army.

The Spanish were fighting the French in a battle in Pamplona, Spain. This area is on the border between the two nations and was long contested. The Spanish were greatly outnumbered, and they retreated to regroup and rethink their strategy. Should they surrender? Flee and return another day with more troops? Ignatius gave one of the great "halftime speeches" in history, stirring his fellow soldiers to fight on for the glory of their king, their nation, and themselves. He was not a general nor even a sergeant—he was a grunt in the trenches with powerful passion and a gift for words. The Spanish charged back into the fray. It was a rout. They lost.

In the battle, Ignatius was struck by a cannonball in the knee and collapsed to the ground in agony. The French were so impressed with his audacity and bravery that they carried him on a stretcher back to his home in Loyola, Spain. Everyone expected him to die.

He was carried to his bedroom in a high corner of his family's castle. A priest gave him the Sacrament of the Anointing of the Sick and Communion and heard his Confession. His family kept vigil with tears and prayers, offering him food and water and medical care from a local doctor. After several brutal surgeries, the leg was set and reset, and incredibly he started to recover. "Our Lord was gradually giving him health, and he was in such a good state that he was cured in all other respects except that he could not hold himself well on his leg, and thus he was forced to be in bed."[1] He would eventually recover, though he would walk with a limp for the rest of his life.

Perhaps you've been in a similar situation, maybe in a hospital or in your own home. You're sick, recovering but still not fully well. You've got time, lots of time, and not much to do. Ignatius asked for books to read. He liked heroic stories of knights and dragons, battles and damsels in distress. Instead, his family brought him a book on the lives of the saints and one on the life of Christ.[2] He was a cultural Catholic and generally familiar with the major saints and the story of Jesus. However, it's less clear how seriously he practiced his faith. Perhaps he was a "ChrEaster" or a "CEO"—going to Mass on Christmas and Easter Only. At this time, for many Spaniards, the glory of Spain and the glory of the Church were closely intertwined. For example, imagine an Italian American who brags that his family has always been Catholic, that he has relatives in Rome, and that his uncle is a bishop. Someone may say, "Wow. You must be really strong in your faith, too." "Well," the man says, "things get busy. I have football season tickets. I don't make it to church every Sunday; it depends on when the game is. And then I'm away on fishing trips most weekends in the spring. So . . ."

As Ignatius read, he paused to look out the window and think about his life: What is important? What isn't? How had he been living his life so far? He thought about reenlisting with the army, with new exploits in battle, and climbing to the upper rungs in the Spanish society. These ideas gave him an initial thrill, but he noticed that later he would feel sad and empty. Then he thought about the lives of the saints. "How would it be if I did this which St. Francis did, and this which St. Dominic did?"[3] These thoughts gave him a sense of joy and hope that continued and did not fade into sorrow later in the day. Slowly, "picking it up from experience that from some thoughts he would be left sad and from others happy, and little by little coming to know the difference in the kind of spirits that were stirring: the one from the devil, and the other from God."[4] In the months ahead, he would pray at shrines and monasteries across Europe. He traveled to Our Lady of Montserrat to venerate an ancient statue of Mary and Jesus. Dramatically, he laid down his sword there. The image is striking: he vowed to serve as a knight for his true Queen and King.

Later, in the *Spiritual Exercises*, St. Ignatius sketches out rules for the discernment of spirits. He used the insights he gained on his sickbed to reflect on the spiritual life. These rules are pithy and practical. He learned these rules the hard way—through his own experiences of injury, self-reflection, and conversion.

"Toward perceiving and then understanding, at least to some extant, the various motions which are caused in the soul: the good motions that they may be received, and the bad that they may be rejected" (*SE*, 313).

CONTEMPLATION: DISCERNMENT OF SPIRITS

What should I do with my emotions, my hopes, fears, and opportunities? I felt these longings, movements, inspirations, and frustrations during my days as a college student, and I continue to feel them as an adult. St. Ignatius wondered where his life would lead, how he could find peace and glory. At first, he believed he could find fulfillment on the battlefield and in the king's castle. After his injury, he saw that lasting peace could be found in the service of Christ: laboring for his kingdom, fighting for the eternal King in the spiritual battles of the human heart. Christ is worth living for and dying for. Yes, "in the beginning there was love." And in the here and now of daily life, things can feel confusing and overwhelming. I need a compass. I need a map to chart the path ahead of me. Better yet, I need a guide— someone who can walk with me and show me where to go.

I'll share a few of Ignatius's rules for discernment of spirits. In essence, the saint talks about consolation and desolation. Consolation is from the Holy Spirit; I should welcome these gifts in my heart and cultivate them with prayer and gratitude. Desolation is from the evil spirit; it is an attack on my heart. I need to notice the work of the evil spirit and defend myself against it as best as I can.

On consolation, Ignatius writes:

> By [this kind of] consolation I mean that which occurs when some interior motion is cause within the soul through which it comes to be inflamed with love of its Creator and Lord. . . . Similarly, this consolation is experienced when the soul sheds tears which move it to love for its Lord – whether they are tears of grief for its own sins, or about the Passion of Christ our Lord, or about other matters directly ordered to his service and praise and service.

> Finally, under the word consolation I include
> every increase in hope, faith, and charity, and
> every interior joy which calls and attracts one
> towards heavenly things and to the salvation of
> one's soul by bringing it tranquility and peace
> in its Creator and Lord. (*SE*, 316)

Part of this description refers to what we might call "obvious
consolation." We experience "love of [our] Creator," "increase
in faith and hope and joy." If you read my first book, you
might think of your Spiritual Top 10 list—these are moments
of great consolation when we experience a warm closeness to
God. These might be special moments in prayer, sacraments
(wedding, ordination), times of wonder at God's glory (looking
at an ocean sunset or a mountain sunrise), or similar events.
Likewise, we see the hearts of Jesus and Mary in joy and peace.
Mary rejoices at the visitation, as she celebrates her miraculous
pregnancy with Elizabeth who is pregnant with John the Baptist.
She sings, "My soul proclaims the greatness of the Lord; my
spirit rejoices in God my savior" (Lk 1:46–47). Jesus "rejoiced
[in] the holy Spirit and said, 'I give you praise, Father, Lord of
heaven and earth'" (Lk 10:21).

Other kinds of consolation may be a bit subtler or unexpected. If I feel "sorrow for sins, or because of the sufferings
of Christ our Lord," I am essentially united with the hearts of
Jesus and Mary. We see Jesus weeping over the sins of Jerusalem
(Lk 19:41). In religious art we see Mary weeping at the foot of
the cross as she beholds her beloved son crucified. In a broken

world, sorrow is the proper response to sin and violence. This is an experience of consolation *if* it draws me closer to the hearts of Jesus and Mary. However, the evil spirit may try to pull me down toward a sense of despair and hopelessness, as we'll see in the next rule.

On desolation, Ignatius writes, "By [this kind of] desolation I mean everything which is contrary . . . obtuseness of soul, turmoil within it, an impulsive motion towards low and earthly things, or disquiet from various agitations and temptations. These move one toward lack of faith and leave one without hope and without love. One is completely listless, tepid, and unhappy, and feels separated from our Creator and Lord" (*SE*, 317). Have you ever felt this way? Have you felt this way today? I have. It doesn't necessarily mean that we have sinned or done something wrong. Desolation is from the evil spirit. Of course he wants to drag me down and away from Jesus. We can resist his efforts. Many saints went through times of desolation in their lives. We are not responsible for experiencing difficult emotions in a time of desolation. We are responsible for how we act in a time of desolation. Our emotions are a kind of signal, indicating our spiritual state. With prayer and practice we can get better at noticing and then properly addressing these feelings.

For example, we see Joseph when Mary tells him that she is pregnant. Initially Joseph falls into desolation. He is confused and upset. Perhaps he feels that Mary has betrayed him. He plans to divorce her quietly. "Such was his intention when, behold, the angel of the Lord appeared to him in a dream and said, 'Joseph, son of David, do not be afraid to take Mary your wife into your home. For it is through the holy Spirit that this child has been conceived in her" (Mt 1:20). Amid his fear and confusion Joseph remains open to the angel's invitation: "Do not be afraid." He resists the fear that nearly overwhelms him. He welcomes Mary and the unborn child Jesus into his life. Conversely, how does Peter respond in his time of desolation? During the Passion of Jesus, three people ask Peter if he is a follower of Jesus. Three times he denies Jesus. After the third time, "the cock crowed, and the Lord turned and looked at Peter. . . . He went out and began to weep bitterly" (Lk 22:60–62). Peter gives in to the sorrow and shame. Instead of welcoming the suffering Jesus, he runs away and mourns his betrayal.

Proper discernment of spirits demands an awareness of our own hearts. In my first book, we walked through several exercises designed to aid us in this "heart knowledge." We ask ourselves, "Am I feeling joyful or sorrowful? Do I feel drawn closer to Christ or is the evil spirit trying to pull me away from him?" Sometimes it's obvious what is happening in my heart. Sometimes I must look deeper. I must listen. I must talk to Christ. I may need a friend, mentor, or pastor to help me.

Once I see where my heart is being pulled, I can take the next step: fruitful action. I'll use a unique image to illustrate: standing on a trampoline with three toddlers. My sister has three young children. They love to go on the backyard trampoline with Uncle Joe. I love it, too. We run, jump, and have competitions. The key for me is to do the opposite of what they do. If they all jump, I stay low. If they fall down, then I can jump. For me, it involves awareness, anticipation, bending my knees, and adjusting to what's happening around me. It's a bit dangerous, fun, and exciting. It's similar in the spiritual life. We can make adjustments to stay upright, responding to our internal state and the events going on around us.

In times of consolation, our response is simple and straightforward: keep going. Thank the Lord for this gift of joy and peace and continue to walk with the Lord. As a savvy guide, Ignatius tells the Christian to "consider how he or she will act in future desolation, and store up new strength for that time . . . to humble and abase herself himself" (*SE*, 323–324). It's as if we are packing for a long journey. We will need food and drink to sustain us, especially in the dry spots that may lie ahead. Jesus tells us to "store up treasures in heaven" (Mt 6:20). Remember. Savor. Thank the Lord. Journaling can help. God blesses me in prayer, through a good conversation with a friend or a beautiful scene in nature. If I write down this graced moment, I can revisit it again later when I'm struggling.

What should we do in times of desolation? "During a time of desolation one should never make a change. Instead, one should remain firm and constant in the resolution and in the decision which one had on the day before the desolation. . . . It is very profitable to make vigorous changes in ourselves against the desolation, for example, by insisting more on prayer, meditation, earnest self-examination, and some suitable way of doing penance" (*SE*, 318–319). Here Ignatius draws on his experience as a soldier: fight back against the enemy. Don't surrender, don't give up, and don't give an inch. In Latin, he uses the phrase *agere contra*, "go against." In desolation, the only change we ought to make is to renew our resolve. Like a military battle, this is typically a brief attack—though it may be fierce and feel like it will never end. Double down. Further, in desolation, Ignatius reminds us that we can resist the enemy's temptations "with God's help, which always remains available" (*SE*, 320). This is a crucial insight. When do people typically wander from God and the Church? It's usually when they are struggling, upset, and confused. They think, "Well, I guess God has abandoned me, so maybe I'll abandon him, too." Giving up means falling right into the devil's trap. "Remain firm and constant in the resolution and decision," says Ignatius. Ask God for help. Turn to a trusted friend for support. Continue your routine of prayer, and even increase it a bit.

This applies to practical decisions, too. Don't quit at the end of your worst day of work. Bring it to prayer. Talk to someone you trust. If appropriate, talk to your boss (after you've calmed down; trust me on this!). Wait until things get better at work and then discern a possible change. Even politics has the phrase "Don't change horses in the middle of a stream"—that is, don't change presidents when there is a war or disaster going on. Resist the devil's temptations and trust that consolation will return soon.

Let's think about this from the devil's perspective. He tempts me. In a difficult moment, he tries to stir up feelings of sorrow, anger, and fear in my heart. He wants to draw me away from Christ. What should I do? Following the wisdom of St. Ignatius, I recommit to prayer. I talk with a trusted friend about my difficulties. I review my journal to recall blessings that God has given me in the past—with a renewed hope that he will bless me again in the future. If appropriate, I go to Confession to acknowledge my failings. What does the evil spirit make of all this? His attack on me has failed. Worse, it backfired. He tried to draw me away from the heart of Christ. Instead, I've taken concrete steps to stay close to Jesus. I've humbly named my own weaknesses, worked against them, and revisited graces from the past. Like a military commander, the devil may cry out, "Halt, you demons! This is a disaster. The more we attack, the more he relies on God. Retreat. Let's find an easier target."

Questions and Exercises

1. Reflect on some patterns in your spiritual life. In your journal, turn to a clean page. On the top of the left page, write "Christ's Words of Truth and Love." Jot down images, words, and people that Christ uses to bless and console you. These may be words you see in the Bible or hear at Mass. Some may be the graces and blessings you have experienced. Example: "I'm made in the image of God." "God is my true Father and Christ is my shepherd." "My grandparents, my children."

2. On the top of the right page, write "Lies of the evil spirit." Jot down some of the temptations, half-truths, and accusations that the devil uses—like arrows shot at your heart. These will very familiar: "I'm not good enough." "The rules don't apply to me." Many of these statements will be irrational. Others, such as, "God won't forgive me," will directly contradict Christian teaching. We want to notice these evil lies and guard our hearts with the shield of faith.

3. What helps me when I'm in desolation? Jot down a few specific actions: a favorite prayer, good habits, taking a walk, talking with a faithful friend, and so forth.

PRAYER FOR GENEROSITY

Lord Jesus, teach me to be generous;
teach me to serve you as you deserve,
to give and not to count the cost,
to fight and not to heed the wounds,
to toil and not to seek for rest,
to labor and not to seek reward,
except that of knowing that I do your will.

—traditional Jesuit prayer

BROKEN HEARTS

I will give you a new heart, and a new spirit
I will put within you. I will remove the heart
of stone from your flesh and give you a heart
of flesh.
—Ezekiel 36:26

The car flipped over ten times, maybe fifteen. I woke up to steel smashing against cement, over and over, over and over. Glass shattered and flew in my face and hair. The sun peeked out from the gray horizon—upside down, then right side up. The car landed on its hood with a final ugly crunch. I had my shoes off in the back seat. The springs under the seat had mangled two toes on my right foot. I found my Chuck Taylor sneakers with the wrap-around American flag design. In a daze of habit, I carefully bent down, pulled them on with no socks, and tied them tight, as blood oozed out from the tongue of my left shoe.1

I stood up. Glass and grit blew into my face as eighteen-wheelers roared by at eighty miles per hour. The red sun cut through the twilight. My sister hugged me, bleeding and screaming. My grandma limped over to check on my grandfather. He was lying face down on the shoulder thirty yards away. He had been thrown from the car. I was in high school. It was more than twenty-five years ago on August 15, the Feast of the Assumption of Mary, when we celebrate Mary being assumed body and soul into heaven at the end of her life on earth.

How do we process pain and loss? It is hard. It takes time. Our body's first reaction is simply shock. Fear freezes us. A disaster happens fast, and it is awful, and it is not in our control. The car is smashed and upside down. My grandma says, "He's dead, he's dead," and hugs us. I hurt everywhere. A dull ache: inside and outside, physically and emotionally. He is gone.

Days later, at home, I missed the first days of my junior year of high school. I was planning to audition for the fall musical at my all-boys Jesuit school. I asked the doctor if I could still run track in the spring. "I don't know," he said. The physical pain was quieting down. Gooey blood congealed into scabs. Most of all, losing my granddad left me feeling like I had a hole in my heart. I remember crying a lot with my sister, mom, dad, and grandma. Sometimes other people, too—friends from school, my youth group, and my cousins.

Tears mean you are alive. Sorrow, especially sorrow that is shared with others, is like a stream that begins to flow through the pain. The stream slowly turns a water wheel that grinds the grit of suffering into flour for bread. Hugging, crying, and talking that sometimes turns into laughter. "Remember when Granddad hooked his ear when we went fishing? And he was wearing that blue denim shirt—he loved that shirt! And his orange truck! Where did he get that truck?"

There is a time for quiet, too. But suffering in silence, trying to tough it out in silence, that is lasting death. Look at a rusted-out factory with brown barbed wire. Without tears, without words, we are petrified.

Over hours and days, my family talked through what happened. Our grandparents had taken us on a trip out West to see the Grand Canyon, the red rock formations in Utah from every cowboy movie, and the sequoias in California. We were driving late, so late it was early, to drop off the rental car and catch a flight. Was there some gravel spilled on the road? Or the steering went out? Or . . .

The Jesuits from my high school came to visit. My youth minister and youth group came to visit. People brought casseroles—so many casseroles! Nine-by-thirteen-inch glass dishes covered with aluminum foil: Italian, breakfast-for-dinner, Mexican, Chinese chicken, even green Jell-O salads. Gifts and offers of more gifts: "If you need anything, let me know." "I can come over again tomorrow if you want." My English teacher offered to let me skip the summer novel that I had put off and put off: "Thanks, Mr. H. That would help me a lot."

We were and are a Catholic family but praying together aloud was not something we had really done, except at Mass and in offering grace before dinner. But in those days, we did pray together aloud. We weren't great at it. Sometimes there were tears, sometimes awkward silence. It helped. I prayed by myself, too. At Mass. Before I went to sleep. I talked to God. I told him I was sad that Granddad was gone. My grandad and I often went fishing, played golf, talked, and went to lunch. And now he was gone. I loved him, and I was grateful for our time together. And I told God that I was mad, too.

The tears and meals, talking and hugging and loving—it all helped me. It unfroze me. Praying with sorrow, gratitude, and anger—this is honest prayer, from the heart. The grit of suffering ground into flour, mingled with salty tears, and now becoming bread. The anger started to fade. Did I want it to fade? Maybe I could hang on to it, keep it going, pour some gas on it, fan the anger flame. But who would that help?

Healing was flowing into my life, slowly yet powerfully. The wounds remained but were not so painful. The scabs dried and peeled off. Soft, sensitive skin lay beneath. A few scars remain. I know I am not the only one with a hole in my heart. When I share this story in a homily or on retreat, people always come up to me afterward: "Father, I've lost someone I love, too." "I have cancer; I know those tears and those casseroles." How can we find healing amid the trauma and loss? "Whoever believes in me, as scripture says: 'Rivers of living water will flow from within him'" (Jn 7:38). The soldier pierced his heart with a lance as he hung on the cross. Out flowed blood and water, the sacraments of the Church. Later, the risen Jesus invited Thomas to touch the wounds.

His wound heals us; grace and mercy pour out of his heart and into mine. Jesus has a hole in his heart. So do I. Maybe you do, too. His love can flow into our hearts, and ours into his, if we let it. He is the bread from heaven. But this bread is won by his Blood, poured out in the chalice at Mass. This is Communion. This is life in Christ: letting others share in our pain, that we may share in his redemption. Then, somehow, we become Eucharistic, a little bit at a time. We receive his Body and Blood into our bodies and blood. Then we can walk with others in their pain so they can walk with him, too. Jesus does not abandon us in times of suffering. Rather, suffering is an invitation to communion with Christ, even in his suffering, and to be embraced by his love.

I saw the sequoias again a few years ago. I love long runs. I do not like long drives. I have granddad's picture on the shelf by my bed, next to an image of the Sacred Heart. He is in his formal army uniform from World War II, smiling. I love him. He loves me. I talk to him. He listens. He was there when I entered the Jesuit novitiate a few years after the accident. He was there when I was ordained a priest. The life of Christ flows in me, from the wound in his heart into the hole in mine. I pray for life with him forever.

OVERVIEW OF THE DAY FROM IGNATIUS: TWO FLAGS

St. Ignatius was a soldier. During his conversion, he came to see that life was a spiritual battlefield. He describes this dramatically in the "Two Standards" meditation in the *Spiritual Exercises*. For our purposes, I'll call it the "Two Flags."

War is chaotic and dangerous. In medieval times, this was especially true. Two armies met on a battlefield. On each side, the standard bearer held the flag representing his king and nation. As the two sides charged, swords clanged, cannons fired, mud spattered, blood spewed, horses reared up, and men fell. Imagine the leader of all the enemy in that great plain of Babylon. Consider how he summons uncountable devils, disperses some to one city and others to another, and thus throughout the whole world. How he admonishes them to set up snares and chains. In contrast, gaze in imagination on the supreme and true leader, who is Christ our Lord. Consider how the Lord of all the world chooses so many persons, apostles, disciples, and the like. He sends them throughout the whole world, to spread his doctrine among people of every state (see *SE*, 138–145).

Pope Francis expands this image when he refers to the Church as a "field hospital."[2] On any battlefield, there are many wounded and suffering people. The Church is called to serve, heal, and minister—even risking our own safety to aid others. As I write this paragraph in early 2022, the world is beginning the third year of the COVID-19 pandemic—with record numbers infected with the omicron variant. The virus has claimed millions of lives globally and infected millions more; it has disrupted everything from family gatherings to sporting events to Catholic Mass. Further, we all feel increasingly discouraged by the tension and animosity regarding mask policies, political confusion, and continued suffering. Precisely here on this battlefield, the Church is called to be a witness of service and mercy.

This battle is not waged on a green grass field in medieval Europe. The war is waged on the whole surface of the earth and in every human heart, including mine. I may need to ask myself a troubling question: "Which side am I on?" The devil sends out evil spirits to "tempt people to covet riches, so that they may more easily come to vain honor from the world, and finally to surging pride" (*SE*, 142). How have these seeds been sown in our hearts? Through media and advertising, our own material successes, or a self-centered vision of the world? How have we given in to these temptations and even tempted others to do the same?

Conversely, "Christ our Lord takes his place in that great plain near Jerusalem, in an area which is lowly, beautiful, and attractive." He calls "to all of his servants and friends whom he is sending on this expedition. He recommends that they endeavor to aid all persons, by attracting them, first to the most perfect spiritual poverty . . . by attracting them to a desire of reproaches and contempt, since from these results humility" (*SE*, 146).

St. Ignatius asks us to pray for the grace of "sorrow, regret, and confusion" as we consider the sins and brokenness of the world and in our own hearts (*SE*, 193). You may be thinking, "Fr. Joe, I am making this retreat to get rid of sorrow and confusion in my life. Why should I ask God for more of those things?"

Sorrow and confusion are the proper responses to sin in the world. We ought to feel these emotions as we look upon our sin and the effects of sin and violence that Jesus experiences in his Passion. In doing so, we're asking for a personal connection with

the person of Jesus. Yes, Jesus suffers and dies for all people—
and for me. Ignatius uses this phrase "for me" a few times in
the *Exercises*. Jesus does this for me. He became man for me,
suffers for me, and dies for me. And he invites me to share in
his sorrows, tears, and suffering (see *SE*, 48).

It takes very little evidence to convince most people that
our world is broken. Sin, violence, evil, and chaos: the proof is
all around us, especially when we look in the mirror.

As I remember my grandfather's death, I still feel sorrow,
confusion, and even anger. Who is responsible? A negligent
road crew? God? Why did this happen? These feelings and questions are natural and reasonable. Feelings of sorrow and loss
are often tied with our experiences of human weakness and
limitations. Most simply, why do people die? This was not part
of God's original plan for the human race. And yet, in a world
wounded by sin, we are mortal; we die. To heal our brokenness,
we must encounter Christ. He is on the battlefield with us, and
he experienced the effects of sin: suffering and death. In his
resurrection, our eternal King triumphs over sin and death.

> I seek to "lower and humble myself, as far
> as is in my power, that in all things I may
> be obedient to the law of God our Lord"
> (*SE*, 164).

CONTEMPLATION:
OUR CALL TO HUMILITY

St. Ignatius knew the violence and chaos of the battlefield. We've all seen war movies—the gunfights of Vietnam and World War II, as well as older battles with swords and horses. Let's focus on the war waged in every human heart, especially our own.

In day 2, we looked at the consolations of the Holy Spirit and the desolations of the evil spirit. As we contemplate the Two Flags, the imagery gets even more vivid and personal. How does the Prince of Darkness try to draw us under his standard? We're asking Christ for the grace to see and understand the evil one's devious strategy so that we can guard our hearts. Ignatius summarizes the evil one's tactics: he will typically "tempt people to covet riches, so that they may more easily come to vain honor from the world, and finally to surging pride." Riches, honor, pride. These goods can seem like shields, insurance, against the brokenness of our hearts and the million broken hearts in the world around us.

Let's unpack the language of these temptations. Some "riches" can be good and useful. A warm house, a functional car, good health: these things can help us to love and serve God and others. God calls us to love people and use things. The evil spirit asks us to use people and love things. He may tempt us to see these things as "ends in themselves." They can become a kind of idol. The pursuit of these goods can be distracting, even all-consuming. For example, a car is an object. It is useful. What if my identity becomes tied up with my car? Maybe I buy a big expensive pickup truck or a flashy convertible—perhaps far more than I can really afford. Or maybe I become obsessed with getting it, even if I don't have it now. "If only . . ."

That is one of the phrases the evil spirit loves to use with us: "If only. . ." "If only I were smarter and better connected. If only I had a more important job . . ." Sometimes it's phrased in the negative: "If only I didn't have this particular weakness, or that problem in my family, or . . ." He loves to use lies and half-truths. He wants us to "covet"—to fixate on some object. Sometimes we covet things that belong to others. "I wish I had his job, his wife, his house." He wants to turn our gaze from Christ the King to objects, whether real or imagined. This is the temptation of Adam and Eve. If only we eat the forbidden fruit, he tells us, "you will be like gods" (Gn 3:5). If we turn away from God, break our relationships, and put all of our hopes in an object, then we'll be "like gods" and truly fulfilled. Here's the thing: We're already like God. God has made us in his image and likeness. What exactly can the devil offer me that God has not already given me?

What is pride and why is it a problem? I want to take pride in my work, don't I? Parents are proud of their children. I am even "proud to be an American," as we hear in the classic song. We should make a distinction between two kinds of pride; I'll distinguish between "grateful pride" and "selfish pride."[3]

Grateful pride puts the focus on God and is a virtue. In this sense, God has given us a gift. We're appreciative, and we want to use it well. A couple that saves to buy a nice house should be proud of their home. In fact, they may feel humbled that God has blessed them with health and income, giving them a comfortable place for their family.

Selfish pride focuses on the individual—"me." Words such as *arrogant* and *prideful* describe this disposition. A proud person tends to see others as mere objects, opportunities, or obstacles for their next triumph.

How does Christ call us to his standard? He invites us to poverty and then to humility. This may seem like a strange marketing strategy for Jesus Inc. Where's the flash and sparkle? Let's dig into humility to find the answer. Humility is not humiliation. In Latin, *humility* is related to the root of *human* and *humus*. What's humus? It's organic material in soil that provides nutrients to all that grows: earth. (That yellow garlicky dip is related to this word; "hummus" looks like clay or mud.) We humans are "from the earth," as we see God shaping our spiritual grandparents in Genesis. To be humble is to be rooted and grounded in our true identity: knowing who we are and who God is. St. Thomas Aquinas writes that humility "consists in keeping oneself within one's own bounds, not reaching out to things above one, but submitting to one's superior."[4] Humility can have a connotation of lowliness—for example, "He comes from a humble background." It also means building our lives on a strong foundation. If I place myself under my superior, God, then I'm guided by his wisdom and love instead of my own opinions and preferences. A humble person does not have an inflated and pride-filled sense of self. Rather they know that

God made them, loves them, and calls them to eternal life. All gifts are from God and should be used to love and serve God and others. Jesus and Mary are humble. The saints are humble. Humble people are a joy to be with. They can listen attentively and speak from the heart. Around humble people I sense, "She really cares about me"; "He's really listening. I can trust this guy."

Thus humility is the golden mean between pride and despair. If selfish pride is having an inflated sense of self ("I'm too good for this"), then despair is having a deflated sense of self. Pride sets us up for a nasty fall into self-loathing, with thoughts such as "I'll never succeed. No one cares about me." Proverbs tells us, "Pride goes before disaster, and a haughty spirit before a fall" (Prv 16:18). Despair is not a Christian virtue. To "love your neighbor as yourself" (Mt 22:39) means that you should love yourself. Jesus loves us and properly loves himself. He knows who he is; his identity is rooted in his relationship with the Father. Jesus takes time for rest, prayer, conversation, and celebration. He does his Father's will and labors in his vineyard for the salvation of the human race. Christian humility lies between the two temptations of pride and despair and transcends them both. We can grow in humility by strengthening our relationship with God. Making a retreat, taking time for prayer, reflecting on the gospels, and writing graces in a journal—these are all good steps toward humility.

Questions and Exercises

1. What are the wounds of your heart that need healing? How have you been wounded by others and the world by sin, violence, and indifference?

2. How have you wounded yourself and others? Through your bad habits, selfishness, sins?

3. How have you damaged your relationship with Christ and the Church?

4. Name one person who has helped you to experience forgiveness, growth, and healing: a pastor, teacher, relative? Jot down a few words describing this moment.

5. Is there anything you wish to say to Jesus or Mary? Anything they wish to say to you?

PRAYER TO LOVE GOD WITH ALL MY HEART

My God, I love thee;
not because I hope for heaven,
nor because I fear the fires of hell.
Thou, O my Jesus,
did embrace me upon the cross;
and did bear for me the nails and spear,
and manifold disgrace.
And griefs and torments and sweat of agony;
even death itself,

and all for me, a sinner indeed.
Then why, O blessed Jesus Christ
should I not love thee well?
not for the hope of winning heaven,
or of escaping hell.
not with the hope of gain,
nor seeking a reward,
but as thyself has loved me,
O ever-loving Lord!
Even so I love thee, and will love thee
and thy praise I will sing,
solely because thou art my God,
and my eternal king.

—St. Francis Xavier, SJ[5]

Pause for Heart Check

You've completed three days of your *Love Him Ever More* retreat. Congratulations! Now is a good opportunity to take a break and do a quick "heart check." This is an opportunity to review what has happened on your retreat so far. What has the Lord been doing? How have you responded? It's like a brief team meeting after the first quarter of a football game or the gathering together of teachers before Thanksgiving break. What are the highlights so far? The lowlights? What's working? What's not?

St. Ignatius recommends that we take time to review our prayer. This helps each of us to "notice and dwell on those points where I felt greater consolation or desolation, or had a greater spiritual experience" (*SE*, 62). What is the Lord doing in our heart? Thank him for these graces! Also, do we need to make any changes before we continue? For example, perhaps I try to pray in bed and I keep falling asleep during prayer!

You could take a few minutes to pause for this heart check at the conclusion of day 3. Or you might choose to do this just before beginning day 4. If you have time, you could take a full day to review the first three days, look through your notes, and savor the graces. Here are a few questions for your prayerful consideration. You may want to jot down a few reflections in your journal.

1. How is your retreat going so far?

2. Are you taking time for daily prayer?

3. Briefly read the reflections you've written in your journal so far.

4. What are a few highlights and graces you've received from the Lord during this retreat?

5. Are there any changes you need to make before you begin day 4?

PART II

HIS HEART:
CENTERED IN CHRIST

DAY 4

HIS HEART, DIVINE AND HUMAN

I will hear what the Divine Persons are saying,
that is, "Let us work the redemption of the
human race." . . . Then I will listen to what
the angel and Our Lady are saying.
Afterwards I will reflect on this, to draw
some profit.
—see *Spiritual Exercises*, 107

My Cub Scout troop went to a fall festival. I was seven years old. We got to carve pumpkins and eat caramel apples. Toward the end of the day, my friend Jason and I went through the "hay bale maze," a huge pyramid of hay bales—stacked up, with twists and turns, ups and downs—decorated for Halloween. We were excited to begin, charged up with sugar and adrenaline. After crawling along for a few minutes, the brightness of the entrance got dimmer and more distant. It was getting dark outside. The setting sun peeked through a few cracks between the bales with fading orange light. We were getting cold. We crawled in, hit a wall, and backed up, stirring up dirt and hay dust. We started coughing. Our initial energy faded with the light. We seemed to hit another wall and had to change course again. "Help, help!" It was a big maze (or seemed that way to a little Cub Scout). If we were in the middle, could anyone even hear us? Would we ever get out? What if the troop left without us? We were crying, coughing, shouting, terrified.

My dad went along on this trip with a few other dads. I remember hearing his voice: "Joe? Where are you?" We shouted louder. What if he couldn't find us? I saw a tiny beam of orange light and reached out my hand through the crack toward the light. "Here, here! I'm right here!" Could he see me or hear me? Just then he grabbed the entire bale of hay, pulled it out, and tossed it aside. He looked huge against the setting sun, as a cloud of dust rose between us. The light and dirt burned our teary eyes. We had hay and dirt in our hair. My dad grabbed me and Jason, lifting us up. We were crying, shivering, tears streaming down our dusty cheeks.

We had gotten into the maze but we could not get out. We needed someone older, bigger, and stronger to rescue us. Someone on the outside who could reach in and pull us to safety. This is the mystery of the Incarnation. The eternal God enters our world to save us. We got ourselves into this mess, but we cannot get ourselves out. Sin, violence, faithlessness—once we fall into this web, we cannot free ourselves. We need a Savior.

On retreats and in spiritual direction, I've worked with people struggling with addictions. Programs such as Alcoholics Anonymous can be a godsend for those who feel trapped by their own poor decisions and chemical dependency. In the 12 Steps of AA, the first step is to "admit that I am powerless over alcohol and that my life has become unmanageable." Maybe it seems odd to begin that way. Powerless and unmanageable? Is that a path to health and sanity? Maybe it is. It is an honest recognition that I need help. However I got into this mess, I can't get out of it alone. I need help, I want help, and I welcome help. It's the dirty little hand reaching out from the darkness into a beam of orange light: "Help!"

The Incarnation is God's supreme act of compassion. God becomes man in Jesus. Even for Christians, when we think about it, this seems impossible. How can the infinite eternal God be contained in a single carpenter in a small town? God sees that we need help and comes to help us. The Incarnation is not something we need to figure out. It's not a math problem: infinity = 1. With the saints, we behold the Incarnation with wonder and love. And with Mary, let us approach with an open heart. We need help. We need a Savior. Let us welcome him and adore him.

OVERVIEW OF THE DAY FROM IGNATIUS: GOD BECOMES MAN

St. Ignatius helps us to reflect on the Incarnation. He invites us to look at three distinct groups of persons. First, we behold the eternal Trinity, looking down on the earth. Second, we see the human race, falling more and more into sin and violence. Third, we see the angel Gabriel greeting Mary (see *SE*, 106).

God says, "Let us work the redemption of the human race." Then we listen to what the angel and Our Lady say. In all of this, I ask for knowledge from God, who became human for me. Yes, God loves everyone. Yes, Jesus comes to draw all people back into communion with the Trinity. And he became out of love for me, as an individual.

> "Ask for an interior knowledge of Our Lord, who became human for me, that I may love him more intensely and follow him more closely" (*SE*, 104).

CONTEMPLATION: OUR SIN AND OUR REDEMPTION

Guided by St. Ignatius, we first looked to the Holy Trinity. "He loves us first," which we examined on day 1 of our retreat. God is three eternal Divine Persons: Father, Son, and Holy Spirit. The Father beholds the eternal Son with infinite love. The Son responds by offering himself to the Father eternally in love. This love between the Father and Son is the Holy Spirit. God exists for all time in glory, power, and love.

Second, we look at the human race. In an act of great love, God has created us. God made the universe, the sun and stars,

the moon and earth. We alone are made in the image and likeness of God (see Genesis 1:26). In the Bible and in human history, we see humanity falling increasingly into sin and division. St.
Ignatius sketches a diverse portrait of humankind for us, seeing
"some white and others black, some in peace and others at war,
some weeping and others laughing, some healthy and others
sick, some being born and others dying" (*SE*, 106).

The sin of Adam and Eve is only the beginning of a long
history of betrayal, violence, and destruction. If you are not sure,
open a history book to any page; you'll likely see wise leaders as
well as treachery and betrayal. Open the newspaper or turn on
the TV news. What happened? How could something so good
turn so bad so fast?

In glory and splendor, God sees the confusion and sinful-
ness of the human race. God looks upon us with a depth of love
and compassion. God does not turn away, does not give up.
God sends prophets, teachers, leaders, and angels. God offers us
commandments, wisdom, forgiveness, and mercy. Finally, God
proclaims, "Let us work the redemption of the human race."
God becomes one of us, one with us. The glorious eternal Son
of God will become the newborn son of Mary.

Third, we turn to Mary. Let's look at the account of the
annunciation in Luke's gospel. There the angel Gabriel appears
to Mary with an incredible invitation: Would she become the
Mother of God?

> "Hail, favored one! The Lord is with you. . . .
> Do not be afraid, Mary, for you have found

favor with God. Behold, you will conceive in
your womb and bear a son, and you shall name
him Jesus. He will be great and will be called
Son of the Most High. . . ." But Mary said to
the angel, "How can this be, since I have no
relations with a man?" And the angel said to
her in reply, "The holy Spirit will come upon
you, and the power of the Most High will over-
shadow you. . . ." Mary said, "Behold, I am the
handmaid of the Lord. May it be done to me
according to your word." Then angel departed
from her." (Lk 1:28, 30–32, 34–35, 38)

In this section, we'll use our imagination to help us engage this
holy scene. Of course, we'll remain within the parameters of
scripture and tradition so as to remain faithful in our prayer.
And we ask for a closer connection, heart to heart, with Mother
Mary and the child Jesus, who became man for us. They have
beating hearts, and so do we.

We'll begin using our sense of sight. Does this scene occur
at daytime or at night? St. Luke does not give us this detail.
Many artists portray this as a night scene—perhaps Mary was
at prayer or awakened from sleep. This likely occurred while
Mary was at home, or perhaps in her parents' home. Using our
physical senses, consider what the weather would have been like.
Nazareth is in Israel, in the Middle East; it is typically sunny and
hot in the daytime, but cool and breezy at night. What about the
smell—a dusty breeze, the scent of approaching rain, or maybe
candles burning? Then let us focus on the appearance of Mary.

She is a young woman, engaged to be married. Look at her face, her eyes, as she beholds this angel. Beneath her expression, consider the emotions in her heart. The gospel tells us that she was "greatly troubled" and "pondered what sort of greeting this might be" (Lk 1:29). She asks, "How can this be?" The angel tells her, "Do not be afraid, Mary." We may get a personal sense of Mary feeling overwhelmed, confused, and yet drawn into this grand vocation. She looks up and slowly exhales, now closing her eyes. God has been with her every day. In the synagogue, she's heard the stories of God's power and might, leading the Jewish people out of slavery, through the Red Sea, and into the Promised Land. She's heard words from the prophets about a Messiah who will come to save us. She's chanted the psalms and pondered them at night: "The LORD is my shepherd; there is nothing I lack" (Ps 23:1). A tear forms in the corner of her eye, rolling down her cheek. "And name him Jesus," says the angel. "Me?" she prays. "You're asking me? Then, yes. *Fiat.* May it be done to me according to your word."

St. John simply writes, "And the Word was made flesh and made his dwelling among us" (Jn 1:14). For the first time, God now takes on human flesh and becomes one of us. In the coming days, the tiny heart of Jesus will begin to beat beneath the heart of Mary as he grows in her womb. God now has a beating human heart. God looks upon the sinful hearts of the human race, seeing our hard hearts. He does not turn away from us. Rather, he offers us his Sacred Heart in his divine child, Jesus.

St. Ignatius also encourages us to "reflect on ourselves." How do you feel as you read and pray with this passage? Joy, hope, fear? Have you ever felt a call from God—and how did you respond? Ignatius then asks us to have a "colloquy," or friendly conversation with the key characters in a gospel passage. Is there anything you want to say to Mary? To ask her? Anything she wants to say to you? Is there anything you want to say to her son, Jesus, as he takes on human flesh as a tiny child in her womb? Take a moment to reflect on this. You may want to jot down a few words and images in your journal or notebook.

The contemplation continues into Mary's visitation of her cousin, Elizabeth. As Mary shares this Good News, Elizabeth's child, John the Baptist, "the infant leaped in her womb, and Elizabeth, filled with the holy Spirit, cried out in a loud voice and said, 'Most blessed are you among women, and blessed is the fruit of your womb'" (Lk 1:41–42). This tiny child, the son of Mary and eternal Son of the Father, brings joy. His Good News is spreading—first to Mary, then to Elizabeth and John. And to Joseph.

Joseph hears two words from Mary that change his life. Mary approaches, touches his hand, and looks him in the eye: "I'm pregnant." She is three months pregnant after visiting Elizabeth; the small bump of her belly confirms her announcement. He looks in her eyes and then looks away. He feels confused and saddened. He may wonder if she has been unfaithful. Perhaps she tries to explain, but it's hard to put into words. "I was praying and then I heard . . . and he me asked if . . . "

Joseph, "unwilling to expose her to shame, decided to divorce her quietly" (Mt 1:19). His dreams of fatherhood and family life are shattered. He loves Mary, proposed to her, she accepted, and now it's over before it began. He prays that night before going to sleep. A tear forms in the corner of his eye, rolling down his cheek. Physically exhausted, he crawls into bed and falls asleep. Then an angel appears to him in a dream: "Do not be afraid. . . . For it is through the holy Spirit that this child has been conceived in her. . . . Name him Jesus" (Mt 1:20, 21). He awakens. Dazed, he looks around the room. He is alone in the dark night. But he wasn't alone and isn't. "Do not be afraid." Easy for angels to say. A light wind blows through the open window. Yellow stars glimmer in the black sky. In the dead of night, Joseph feels quiet and peace; calm and clear like the sky. "Jesus." No one in his family has that name. What would people say? They would surely notice his fiancée's pregnancy; even his relatives in other cities could do the simple math: "Joseph, when were you married? And the boy was born in late December, wasn't he?" "Name him Jesus." Well, who cares what they think?

Joseph "did as the angel of the Lord had commanded him and took his wife into his home" (Mt 1:24). He finds her, looks her in the eye, and touches her hand. "Mary, I love you and want you as my wife. There's just one thing. I know what we should name the child." She smiles and says, "Jesus."

With Joseph and Mary, we are called to walk on this grand journey of salvation. The path will have many twists and turns. Yet, we know that we travel with Christ Jesus.

Questions and Exercises

Now it's your turn! Use Ignatian contemplation to pray with
the Nativity. Choose one scene from Matthew 1–2 or Luke 1–2
(Joseph and Mary's journey to Bethlehem, arrival of the three
kings, etc.).

1. Imagine the place. Use your five senses. Consider the
   climate, time of day, setting.

2. See the people. What does Mary look like? Her clothing and
   face? What is Joseph's expression, disposition, and emotion-
   al state? What are they saying?

3. Place yourself in the scene "just as if you were there," writes
   Ignatius. See yourself as a humble servant, eager to assist the
   Holy Family. Maybe ask to hold Mary's hand or to touch the
   face of the child Jesus.

4. Conclude with a conversation with Jesus, Mary, or Joseph,
   "as one friend speaks to a friend, or a servant to a leader." Is
   there anything they want to say to you? Jot down a few key
   words and images.

5. Close with a familiar prayer—for example, Our Father or
   Hail Mary.

PRAYER TO THE CHRIST CHILD

O Little Infant Jesus, my only treasure,
I abandon myself to Your every wish.
I seek no other joy than that of calling forth Your sweet
  smile.
Grant me the graces and the virtues of Your Holy
  Childhood,
so that on the day of my birth into Heaven
the angels and saints may recognize me as truly Yours.
—St. Thérèse of Lisieux[1]

HIS HEART CALLS TO MY HEART

I no longer call you slaves, because a slave
does not know what his master is doing.
I have called you friends, because I have
told you everything I have heard from
my Father.
—John 15:15

"Hey, kid, you're trespassing. You can't stay here."

I woke up, half asleep on the bench of a big tractor. It was cool, dark, and breezy in the big barn. "Okay. Sorry. I'll go." I grabbed my backpack and squinted toward the sun pouring through the open barn door. The beams refracted in his aviator sunglasses. I stood up, wobbly. I nodded and forced a half smile, and walked toward the door. Where would I sleep that night?

Jesuits make a pilgrimage as part of their formation. This journey is rooted in the life of St. Ignatius. In 1521, he was

injured by a cannonball blast and walked with a limp for the
rest of his life. At the age of thirty, he had a profound conversion. He then walked from Spain to Rome, praying, begging,
and serving. He caught a boat to Jerusalem so that he could see
where Jesus himself lived and walked.

Jesuit pilgrimage has taken different shapes over the centuries. Some have journeyed to cathedrals and shrines. A few have
traveled to Loyola, Spain, the birthplace of St. Ignatius. In recent
decades, some Jesuit superiors have reimagined this trip for a
modern context. All Jesuits make the thirty-day silent retreat
during our first year in the novitiate. After that, we are asked
to pray about a journey to which God is calling us to. We each
had to present a proposal to the superior for approval. I noticed
that in Ignatius's journey, he often spoke with leaders in the
Church and European society. Sometimes this was accidental,
and sometimes quite deliberate. It was the beginning of the
Reformation. The European Church was a mix of saints and
scoundrels, with some Catholics laboring for authentic renewal
and others mired in corruption. Ignatius spoke with dukes, bishops, princesses, and professors to cooperate in Church renewal.
We don't have queens or dukes in America today. Who shapes
our culture, opinions, and values? In prayer, one name came to
my mind: Oprah.

It was the spring of 2001. I was twenty-three. Oprah Winfrey
was one of the most popular personalities on TV. I had glanced
at her show a few times. She was smart, wealthy, successful—an
American version of the duchesses that Ignatius spoke with.

She clearly had a generous heart. She had given away millions to different charities. If I could talk with her, what would I say?

I had been involved in the pro-life club when I was in college. I had walked in the annual March for Life in Washington, DC, in January 2000, entering the Jesuits just a few months later. On my thirty-day retreat, I had experienced a special closeness to Jesus and Mary, especially at the Nativity. My name is Joseph. What if Oprah took on a major role in the pro-life movement? I hadn't heard her say much on this topic, and I wasn't sure of her beliefs. Her religious views were cryptic. She was raised Christian and occasionally mentioned Jesus amid references to psychology.

I game-planned this with a Jesuit friend. He told me, "Okay, one in ten chance that you shake hands with her. One in a hundred you get one minute with her. One in a million she invites you to coffee and you talk for an hour." Even getting permission felt like a slim chance. I asked: "Fr. Mike, I want to go to Chicago . . . and try to talk with Oprah." Fr. Mike raised his brown eyebrows: "Oprah. Hmm. I've had guys try to meet Elie Wiesel and Maya Angelou. I guess we can give it a shot." Fr. Mike handed me thirty-five dollars and said, "Call me if you get in trouble. And don't get in trouble." I ordered a one-way bus ticket and packed my small backpack. I'd be on the road for a month.

I climbed onto the Greyhound bus. It was late April in Minnesota, where the Jesuit novitiate is located. Up north, it's still late winter in April, with slushy gray snow piles on every corner. I rode the bus to the University of Wisconsin in Madison. St. Ignatius spent time at the University of Paris after his conversion, meeting Francis Xavier and drawing him into the early Jesuits. I wanted to meet some students and do a little vocation promotion before I started walking the ninety miles to Milwaukee.

"Wanna throw a Frisbee?" and "Hey, can I fill up my water bottle?" These became my two main conversation starters. Then I'd wait as the rest of the conversation took unexpected turns. I stepped on campus and zipped my sweatshirt against the April chill. "Sure. I'll throw." Backpacks dropped as I grabbed my white plastic Frisbee. I tossed, he caught, and tossed to me. I caught and tossed. "Nice day," I said. The student seemed interested and puzzled as I described my journey. He offered to walk me to the Catholic Newman Center to find someone who could help me.

We arrived. "Jesus rocks" was painted in yellow poster paint on the front window. After a short conversation, four male students agreed to host me on the floor of their apartment for a few days. I promised to pay rent by washing their dishes. I went on a retreat that weekend and gave a short testimony about my trip. Students gave me a few dollar bills and pizza coupons. I told them about my plan to walk to Milwaukee. Without camping gear I'd need to find a place to stay each night.

I walked on the Glacial Drumlin State Trail and covered fifteen to twenty miles each day. I had time to pray, write, and think. I had a rosary: Jesus and Mary, traveling with Joseph.

Perhaps I was the same age as Joseph when the angel spoke to him in dreams, sending him all over Israel to protect the newborn King. As afternoon turned to evening, I walked up to a house, took a deep breath, knocked, and smiled: "Hi."

"Hey, man, what can I do for you?"

"Can I fill up my water bottle? I can just use your garden hose here if that's okay."

"Sure, no problem. I'll take it inside and get you some ice. Are you camping?"

"Yeah, kind of."

"Be right back."

I took another deep breath.

"Here you go. Which way are you heading?"

"Milwaukee."

"Wow, you've got a ways to go. Where's your tent?"

Deep breath. Smile. "Thanks. Actually, I'm on a pilgrimage. I'm a seminarian and I . . ."

I finish my story after two minutes.

"Hmm. So you're looking for a place to stay tonight. My wife would kill me if I bring you inside. What about the garage? We've got a couch out there. I can grab some blankets, maybe a sandwich or a granola bar."

"Sounds great. Thank you."

I sat on the couch and pulled off my boots, hot and sweaty, and inspected several blisters that were starting to form. He handed me a Coke, a plate with a ham sandwich, and a bag of chips. I smiled. I consumed all of it in less than a minute, about

5 percent of what I could've eaten right then. Maybe Joseph felt this way; no room at the inn. Just a sandwich and chips. But not bad, really. A warm safe garage, with Jesus and Mary beside me.

Over the next week I continued my walk. One night, a janitor at a parish paid for me to stay in a hotel room, since the rectory was locked. "Priest is out of town." In another spot, an older pastor let me stay with him one night. "I don't know what your superior is thinking. This sounds crazy. Hope you make it." And more importantly: "Help yourself to the fridge. Whatever you want." He went to a meeting. I made a twelve-egg omelet with cheese and a whole pack of fried bacon. I stuffed it all into a loaf of French bread. For the first time that week, I felt full.

Along the way I wrote Oprah postcards. I had designed a few with a map of Wisconsin, using our novitiate copy machine and some blue cardstock. "Ms. Winfrey! I'm almost in Milwaukee! Hoping to be in Chicago next week. I'd love to chat for a minute if you are free. Prayers promised. Here's my email . . ." It was a long shot.

I didn't get to meet her. I did get in to see her show. I was the only one in black clerics in an audience of mainly women wearing pastel colors. Along the way I had volunteered in several women's shelters and pro-life pregnancy centers. I talked with the women on staff and learned from them. I helped fold and sort baby clothes. I met a woman named Vicki Thorn, who founded Project Rachel, a ministry of healing and reconciliation for women who have had an abortion. She and her husband have welcomed dozens of foster children into their

Milwaukee home. When I got back to Minnesota, I had almost $300 in cash—donations above and beyond my expenses for food and shelter. And in my mailbox I saw a yellow envelope from Harpo Studios, Oprah's office. "Dear Joseph, I'm sorry that Ms. Winfrey was not available to meet with you. Please accept this autographed photo as a memento . . ."

Jesus is my friend. I had plenty of time to listen and talk with him on my pilgrimage. At times, I could feel him speaking and working through others—feeding me, housing me, encouraging me. I sensed him speaking through me when I talked with Boy Scouts, pregnant women, and faithful families. Yes, he calls me as a disciple and as a vowed religious, but this flows from a primary relationship with him. He calls me his friend.

OVERVIEW OF THE DAY FROM IGNATIUS: FRIENDSHIP WITH JESUS

Jesus calls us his friends. Jesus becomes man and walks among us. Perhaps we presume that he will be simply an example for us: "Watch what I do." He is a model for us and he invites us to do more and to become more with him. He wants us to be his friends. "I no longer call you slaves . . . . I have called you friends" (Jn 15:15). He wants to be in relationship with us—with me, with you. He speaks to us and listens to us. He knows us and wants to be known by us. St. Ignatius initially named the Jesuit order the Companions of Jesus. In Spanish, *companion* literally means "with bread" (*con* = with, *pan* = bread). We walk with

Jesus, we talk with him, and he feeds us with the Bread of Life: himself. Contemplating the risen Jesus, St. Ignatius asks us to

> Consider the office of consoler which Christ our Lord carries out, and compare it with the way friends console one another. (*SE*, 224)

> Love consists in a mutual communication between two persons. That is, the one who loves gives and communicates to the beloved what he or she has, or a part of what one has or can have; and the beloved in return does the same to the lover. (*SE*, 231)

Ignatius uses the image of a human relationship—a good marriage or a close friendship—to describe how we should relate to God. Sharing gifts mutually. Further, this is a symbol of "giving themselves" mutually—in care, support, and affirmation. We may see this kind of love at work in the relationship that Jesus has with the Father.

"Everything that the Father has is mine" (Jn 16:15) and "the Father loves the Son and has given everything over to him" (Jn 3:35). This can make us uncomfortable. We may prefer that Jesus stay up high and far away, giving us teachings and commands. Certainly he teaches us. And he comes down the mountain to walk with us, to speak with us face to face. There are hints of this in the Old Testament. "Do not fear, for I have redeemed you; I have called you by name: you are mine. When you pass through waters, I will be with you" (Is 43:1–2). And "LORD, you have probed me, you know me: you know when I sit and stand; you understand my thoughts from afar" (Ps 139:1–2).

Jesus spent time with Mary, Martha, and Lazarus. They are brother and sisters. This seems to be downtime for Jesus; he's not "on duty" around them but simply relaxing with friends.

How does Christ speak to us now? How does he call us? How do we respond to Christ's call? Let's look at the call of St. Peter: how Christ works with him, speaks with him, and how Peter responds.

> As Christ has given himself to me, so I desire to give myself to him (see *SE*, 234).

CONTEMPLATION: THE CALL OF PETER

Let's use the tools of Ignatian contemplation to imagine this scene. "While the crowd was pressing in on Jesus and listening to the word of God, he was standing by the Lake of Gennesaret" (Lk 5:1).

Jesus is preaching, and the crowd is loving it. He is moving them to laughter, sorrow, wonder, and prayer. The mustard seed, the prodigal son, the Good Shepherd.

Perhaps it is morning. People are coming to the market, running some errands, and here is this preacher in the right place at the right time—offering humor, wisdom, prayer, and something more that they can't quite put their finger on. They've seen him before, heard a few lines in passing. As the crowd grows, more wander over in curiosity: What's going on here?

A few fishermen are near the shore. They're finishing a long night of work, ready to get a bite to eat and then go to sleep. In their tiredness, they're half listening to this carpenter, smiling at a few of his lines, thinking about others, but mainly looking forward to going home. As the crowd spreads around, they're suddenly part of the audience.

"He saw two boats there alongside the lake; the fishermen had disembarked and were washing their nets. Getting into one of the boats, the one belonging to Simon" (Lk 5:2).

Jesus gets into Simon Peter's boat. He does not ask permission. "Put out a short distance from the shore," Jesus asks (Lk 5:3). Part of his request is practical. Jesus is a fine public speaker. He needs to get some space between himself and the crowd so that his voice can carry the Word more widely. Water is the perfect amplifier. He sails out a bit, they stay close to shore; he can see them, and they can hear him.

Peter is ready for a meal and a nap. He's sweaty, dirty, and tired. And the cool of the morning slowly turns into the midday heat. The sun rises and burns off the dawn mist. Some of us fish as a hobby. For Peter, this is his profession—a job he does six days a week. Actually, six nights per week. Fishermen work at night. Exhausted, he's been half listening to this carpenter from Nazareth. And he's curious. "Okay, men. You heard him. Let's row out in the water, just a bit." Groans, and the slosh of oars in the water.

"Then he sat down and taught the crowds from the boat" (Lk 5:3).

More preaching, now at a higher volume, with crowds bigger still. Peter has a front-row seat. He can see Jesus's eyes, his hand gestures, the sweat on his brow. "The kingdom of heaven is like a net thrown into the sea, which collects fish of every kind" (Mt 13:47). After he had finished speaking, he turned to Simon, "Put out into deep water and lower your nets for a catch" (Lk 5:4).

Imagine yourself next to Peter: hot, tired, hungry, sweaty, dirty. Jesus looks you in the eye with great love. He knows you, even as he knows Peter. "Put out into deep water."

It's noon. The Middle Eastern sun blazes overhead. Peter has already gone an extra mile for this man—going back on the water at the end of his long work night. Now Jesus wants more? Simon said in reply, "Master, we have worked hard all night and have caught nothing" (Lk 5:5). It's obvious to everyone, but Peter names the situation: he is hot, tired, hungry, and has nothing to show for his work. He looks up at the yellow sun, then into the dark water, and then back at Jesus. He thinks it over for a moment, and says, "At your command I will lower the nets" (Lk 5:5).

A groan from his workers: "Are you kidding me? We want to go home! Why are you listening to this guy?" How do you respond?

They had just washed the nets. Now they'll drop them back into the dark water—maybe dragging through seaweed or a sunken ship, necessitating more cleaning and repairs. Because no professional fisherman or hobbyist expects to catch fish under the noon sun—in the daytime, the fish go down deep where it is cool, far from their rope nets—this feels like madness and a waste of time.

"When they had done this, they caught a great number of fish, and their nets were tearing. They signaled to their partners in the other boat to come to help them. They came and filled both boats so that they were in danger of sinking" (Lk 5:6–7).

Jackpot. After years of patient work, with a few bad nights and a few good ones and many more in between, this is it. Hand over hand, pulling in the nets, smiling, laughing, sweating, rejoicing. This is the catch of a lifetime. They may not be set for life, but their food and money are set for the year. And like all fishermen, bragging rights for this day will last forever: "Simon, tell it again. Tell us about that day at noon with the carpenter. And, John, you were there, too! A few of you haven't heard this story; you'll never believe it!"

The men rejoice, but something different happens in Peter's heart. He's won the lottery and suddenly he wants to cry. "When Simon Peter saw this, he fell at the knees of Jesus and said, 'Depart from me, Lord, for I am a sinful man.' For astonishment at the catch of fish they had made seized him and all those with him, and likewise James and John, the sons of Zebedee, who were partners of Simon" (Lk 5:8–9).

James and John feel it, too. This was not luck. This man Jesus knows them, knows their hearts. It's as if he knows their thoughts.

"Jesus said to Simon, 'Do not be afraid; from now on you will be catching men.' When they brought their boats to the shore, they left everything and followed him" (Lk 5:10–11).

"Follow me." Jesus says this to Levi as he sits by the custom's post. "He got up and followed him" (Lk 5:28). "Follow me." Peter, James, and John hear his invitation. They follow him.

He looks you in the eye: Follow me. He calls us as his friends and disciples. He calls us to follow him. He calls us to himself, to be with him. Yes, we are laborers in the vineyard with him, servants of the eternal King. Yes, we are called to follow the commandments, as Jesus does himself. And, he says, "I call you friends." He wants us to walk with him. "It was not you who chose me, but I who chose you and appointed you to go and bear fruit" (Jn 15:16). "As the Father loves me, so I also love you. Remain in my love" (Jn 15:9). God is love. Jesus loves us, and he wants to spend time with us. He treasures being with us. He became man to be with us: "I chose you."

This abundant catch echoes throughout the gospels and the Church. Three loaves and a few fish feed five thousand. Peter's boat groans under the weight of the massive catch. The Church, too, swells with every new baptism, every conversion, as one or two or five thousand more offer their hearts to the heart of Christ.

Perhaps our friendship with Jesus is like this story. At first maybe we were hesitant, reluctant, unsure. We've seen Jesus around, heard him and thought about him. Some Christians feel like they are "going through the motions," going to church regularly, saying prayers, but somehow distant from Jesus. Then we hear his invitation. This may occur in a moment of prayer, through a friend, or in a time of sorrow. Perhaps this call came at an unexpected or inconvenient time: "Come and follow me." We may resist and protest for a while: "I'm busy, tired, and hungry." He persists. "Follow me. I call you friends." The lives of many saints follow this trajectory. They hear his call, respond, and nothing is the same afterward. In him, their lives produce fruit that is thirty, or sixty, or ninety times more than they imagined. In Christ, we know that God has great plans for us, too. He calls us to himself as friends and disciples.

Questions and Exercises

It's your turn again! Use Ignatian contemplation to pray with a passage from the ministry of Jesus. You may want to focus on a scene where Jesus heals a sick person or when he calms the storm at sea. I'll suggest one: Jesus dines with Martha, Mary, and Lazarus (John 12). This occurs days after Jesus raised Lazarus from the dead.

1. Imagine the place. Use your five senses. Smell the fragrant oil. What food is being served? Consider the lighting, arrangement of the room, and more.

2. See the people. For example, Mary, a close friend of Jesus, took a liter of perfumed oil and "anointed the feet of Jesus and dried them with her hair" (Jn 12:3).

3. Place yourself in the scene "just as if you were there": at table with Jesus, eager to listen and help.

4. Conclude with a conversation with Jesus or one of the people in the scene, "as one friend speaks to a friend, or a servant to a leader." Is there anything they want to say to you? Jot down a few key words and images.

5. Close with a familiar prayer: Anima Christi, Suscipe, etc.

PRAYER TO CHRIST THE KING

Eternal Lord of all things,
I make my offering with your favor and help,
I make it in the presence of your infinite goodness,
And of your glorious Mother
and of all the holy men and women
in your heavenly court
I wish and desire, and it is my deliberate decision,
provided only that it for your greater service and praise,
is to imitate you in bearing all injuries and affronts
and any poverty, actual as well as spiritual,
if your Most Holy Divine Majesty desires
to choose and receive me into such a life and state.

—*Spiritual Exercises*, 98

HIS BODY AND BLOOD, MINGLED WITH MINE

As I went up to receive Him in Holy
Communion, He showed me His
Sacred Heart as a burning furnace.
—St. Margaret Mary Alacoque, VHM[1]

A young woman prays quietly, kneeling at a wooden pew in a cool stone chapel.[2] It's a night like many others. The December chill slides through the wooden windowpanes. The chapel is quiet with the aroma of candle wax and incense from the Christmas celebrations. She turns the pages of a small prayer book, glancing up at the crucifix over the main altar. She suffers from occasional stress and has trouble sleeping. She can speak with a few friends about these issues and find support. Others find her a bit odd. She is friendly, clumsy, and a bit nervous. And there is something else. She's never been able to name it. A stirring.

A hope and desire for something, for someone. She feels it now. She hears something in the dark, quiet at first but getting louder and more insistent. And sees something. Sees someone. Sees him. "Behold the heart."

Is she sleeping? Dreaming? Seeing things? "Behold."

No. She wasn't seeing. She was seen.

"Behold the heart."

She was not beholding. Someone was beholding her. She heard, "Behold the heart that has loved men so much." The heart that has loved *you* so much.

Over several weeks and months, Sr. Margaret Mary Alacoque, VHM, would see visions of the Sacred Heart of Jesus in her convent chapel many times. In her journal she describes seeing his heart, pierced and bleeding, with flames coming from it and a crown of thorns around it. He told her to behold his heart, which so loved humanity. Then he seemed to take her heart and place it in his heart. In return he gave her back part of his flaming heart.[3]

Contemporary images of the Sacred Heart are rooted in the revelations received by St. Margaret Mary. Painters depict the light, the crown of thorns, and the fire of his love in his heart pierced. Sometimes he came to her with very specific instructions: "Honor My Sacred Heart on the first Friday of each month. Tell your sisters." And "Pray before the Eucharist for one hour on Thursday night—the night before you honor me on first Fridays."

She later reflected:

> This Divine Heart is an ocean of all blessings,
> and into it the poor should submerge all their
> needs.
> It is an ocean of joy in which all of us can
> immerse our sorrows.
> It is an ocean of lowliness to counteract our
> foolishness,
> an ocean of mercy for the wretched,
> an ocean of love to meet our every need.[4]

When she talked with her community, she was met with a mix of reactions. Curiosity and belief, eye rolls and disbelief. She spoke with her superior who was not sure what to make of all this. Her superior reached out to a young Jesuit priest. Fr. Claude de La Colombière, SJ, had been chaplain to the king of England. However, due to shifting alliances and political maneuvers, Fr. Claude was persecuted, imprisoned, and banished from England. He arrived at the French village sick and exhausted. People quickly saw his wisdom and faithfulness. Maybe he could help this young sister. Maybe he could make sense of this.

After a few conversations, Fr. Claude was convinced that these visions were from Christ himself. These visions were consistent with the faith of the Church, with scripture and tradition. In fact, there was nothing new here at all. The essence of her prayer experience was this: "Jesus loves me. He loves all of us. He wants us to love him and others." Yet he was speaking and revealing this message in a unique and powerful way. He was asking her to spread this message. As a cloistered nun, she had a limited social circle: her community, occasional letters, and a few friends and family members who came to visit her. Jesus later asked Sr. Margaret Mary to tell Fr. Claude to preach this message as well. Thus Claude became a great apostle of the Sacred Heart—through his homilies, retreats, and writings—spreading this devotion around France and beyond. In one of his journals, St. Claude wrote:

> This heart is still the same, always burning with love for us, always open so as to shower down graces and blessings upon us, always touched by our sorrows, always eager to impart his treasures to us and to give himself to us, always ready to receive us, to be our refuge, our dwelling place, and our heaven even in this world.[5]

Sr. Margaret Mary's visions began on December 27, 1673, and continued for eighteen months. At this time, France was slowly changing from a rural medieval culture to a complex modern society. These ripples of change shook the foundations of the French Church.

The serpent of Jansenism snaked through many French cities around this time. Jansenism was eventually condemned as a heresy, but it took time for Church officials to recognize its dangerous message. Initially it seemed to be a form of Catholic renewal—calling people to live their faith and morals in an upright and vigorous way. Yet gradually Jansenist priests and preachers began cautioning people about going to Communion, telling them that we offended God when we received the Body of Christ into our sinful bodies. Jansenism is now considered a heresy because it taught that there was an infinite chasm between the depravity of human nature and the perfection of God. Authentic Christian doctrine teaches that Jesus Christ bridges this chasm.

The Sacred Heart devotion was taken up by Fr. Claude and other Jesuits around France to counteract Jansenist preachers. These Jesuits taught that we are sinners and that Jesus Christ truly does love us. Jesus gives us his heart. He wants us to spend more time before the Eucharist, not less. He calls us to honor him by coming to Mass more often, not less; honoring him on First Fridays as well as Sundays and on additional feasts and solemnities. Of course, he calls us to Confession; we should not receive the Eucharist if we are in a state of mortal sin. But the Eucharist is a spiritual food that brings healing, forgiveness, and nourishment.

OVERVIEW OF THE DAY FROM IGNATIUS: CHRIST ABIDES IN US

St. Ignatius writes, "He instituted the most holy sacrifice of the Eucharist as the greatest sign of his love. 'Take and eat,' he told them" (*SE*, 289). Christ gives us himself. "Take and eat; this is my body" (Mt 26:26). He wants to abide in us, to renew us from within. He desires a depth of communion with us, sharing his life, love, wisdom, and grace with us. In the Eucharist, it is as if his blood can now course through our veins. His Sacred Heart beats at the center of the Body of Christ, the Church.

He abides in us and invites us to abide in him. In his Sacred Heart, there is a mutual abiding, in fact. Or to put it another way, we are invited to abide in the heart of Christ! *Abide*—what does this word mean? I abide in an abode, a home. My home is with him, my home is in him. My heart is at home in his heart. Our hearts are restless until they rest in thee, Lord.

St. Ignatius refers to the Eucharist as the "greatest sign of his love for us." Jesus offers himself to us—in the Incarnation, in the Eucharist, in a retreat, in our families and friends, in the Church. He seeks only a welcome, that he may abide in our hearts. The Eucharist is the culmination of his mission throughout the gospels. Jesus shares this holy plan with us through many images in the gospels: "Behold, I stand at the door and knock" (Rv 3:20). "Whoever receives me receives the one who sent me" (Jn 13:20). "I am the vine, you are the branches. Whoever remains in me and I in him will bear much fruit, because without me you can do nothing. . . . As the Father loves me, so I also love you. Remain in my love" (Jn 15:5, 9). To remain in his heart, to abide in his heart, as he seeks to abide in our hearts—this is the prayer of St. Margaret Mary, and it's our prayer, too.

Let us recall from the previous day that Christ calls us friends. He wants to be with us, to spend time with us—even as we enjoy being with our own friends. In this contemplation, we will seek to enter the upper room with Jesus and his disciples at the Last Supper. On this night, Jesus institutes the

Eucharist—offering us his body and blood. We ask to place ourselves there with him. We are his friends and disciples, too. He wants us there. He wants us there each Sunday, and even more often for those who are able—on First Fridays, on feast days, and more. Again, we will engage our five senses—seeing, hearing, touching, tasting, smelling. Further, we ask to engage our emotions, offering our hearts to abide in Christ's heart in this holiest of nights. In this meditation, we'll use our imaginations as well as another technique recommended by St. Ignatius: "Contemplating the meaning of each word of a prayer." One should "consider the word as long as meanings, comparisons, relish, and consolations connected with it are found" (*SE*, 252). We'll use the four words we hear at every Mass: *took, blessed, broke, gave.*

Christ dwells in me, "giving me existence, life, sensation and intelligence; even further, he makes me his temple, since I am created in a likeness and image of the Divine Majesty. Then once again I will reflect on myself" (*SE*, 235).

CONTEMPLATION:
THE LAST SUPPER
AND THE EUCHARIST

Jesus offers us the Eucharist at the Last Supper. Briefly, let's consider the wider setting of this Passover celebration in the scriptures and in Jewish life. Throughout, we'll keep our attention on his Sacred Heart. We want to reflect on his thoughts and emotions in this final meal before his Passion and Death.

Jesus sees the storm clouds gathering. Increasingly the Pharisees' hearts are hardened. They are plotting with the Romans to put an end to this prophet Jesus once and for all. In Matthew's gospel, Jesus prepares for his Last Supper. As he gathers with his closest friends for the Passover celebration, he knows that one of them will betray him. Matthew writes:

> The disciples then did as Jesus had ordered, and prepared the Passover. When it was evening, he reclined at table with the Twelve. . . . While they were eating, Jesus took bread, said the blessing, broke it, and giving it to his disciples said, "Take and eat; this is my body." Then he took a cup, gave thanks, and gave it to them, saying, "Drink from it, all of you, for this is my blood of the covenant, which will be shed on behalf of many for the forgiveness of sins. I tell you, from now on I shall not drink this fruit of the vine until the day when I drink it with you new in the kingdom of my Father." Then, after

> singing a hymn, they went out to the Mount of
> Olives. (Mt 26:19–20, 26–30)

This is the Jewish Passover celebration, one of the most solemn events of the year. Annually they recall God leading them out of slavery and into the Promised Land. Through Moses, the great prophet, God leads his people through the Red Sea, into the desert, feeding them with manna amid storms, plagues, and dangers.

For Jews and for Christians, this is also an image of God freeing us from sin and death. Providing for us in the journey of life and into eternal life amid our own fears, dangers, and temptations. Jesus leads his disciples, us, in prayer during this solemn celebration of Passover. He gathers us at this table—with wine, unleavened bread, bitter herbs, and roasted lamb. At this celebration he offers himself, his life, his heart, his Body and Blood to us in an everlasting sacrifice, to free us from sin and death.

During his time of ministry, he spends a lot of time with the Twelve, talking, praying, eating, walking. He is forming them, teaching them, shaping them. These will be the first bishops and leaders of the early church. As Jesus preaches, teaches, and heals, they will do the same after Pentecost.

Let Christ draw us into this solemn moment. Let us see the candles burning, smell the aromas of the meal, and look at the faces of the disciples. He looks at us now with great love and a sense of sorrow. One of us will betray him. Judas betrays him when he hands Jesus over to the Pharisees and high priests. Peter also denies Jesus three times before the rooster crows at dawn. All the apostles are scattered in fear. What about us? How are we tempted to back away from Jesus, to succumb to fear? Only John remains with him to the end, beholding him at the foot of the cross, standing next to Mother Mary and Mary Magdalen.

What does Jesus do? He takes the bread and says, "Take this all of you and eat of it, for this is my body, given up for you." He gives himself. He offers his heart. This is what he's done—in the Incarnation, God becoming man for us. He offers himself in his words, actions—preaching, healing, friendship, love. He gives his heart. He does so now in a deeper and more dramatic way, offering truly his Body and Blood in the Eucharist to the disciples, to us.

St. John offers us a brief and powerful detail. It is one that we can easily overlook. One of his disciples, the one whom Jesus loved, was reclining at Jesus' side" (Jn 13:23). St. John is the beloved disciple. He is sitting next to Jesus, and in a loving gesture, he places his head on Jesus's heart. You've probably seen a child do this, leaning their head on their father's chest. John is the youngest disciple. Jesus is a spiritual father to him. Let us behold this gesture and ask to enter into it in prayer. We, too, are beloved disciples of Jesus. He, too, invites us to sit next to him, close to him. As he invites us into this warm embrace, may we hear the beat of his Sacred Heart; the gentle, powerful rhythm of his love, poured out moment by moment, on this dramatic and dangerous evening.

Let us consider four words that we hear at every Mass, to savor the "meanings, comparisons, relish, and consolations" that Christ offers us.[6]

Took. Jesus takes bread. He has chosen this particular bread to become Eucharist. Jesus is uniquely taken by the Father. He is the eternally begotten Son, God from God, Light from Light. He was set apart before time began. And the Father takes him, plunging him into the grand mission of the Incarnation. We see this in his baptism, in the Transfiguration, and when he multiplies the loaves and fishes. Jesus takes this bread to transform it into his Body in the Eucharist.

How have you been "taken" and set apart by God? Perhaps this occurred at a young age. When did you first have a sense that God may be calling you to himself in a special way, to abide with him? As Christians, we are the chosen people of God. This should not fill us with a sense of superiority but rather humility and trust. God prepares us for a special mission.

Blessed. Jesus blesses this bread, calling down the Holy Spirit to transform it into his Body in the Eucharist. He does this at every Mass. Truly Jesus is blessed by the Father. He is God from God and Light from Light. "This is my beloved Son, with whom I am well pleased," the Father proclaims from heaven (Mt 3:17). The Father pours out his life, his love, his very being in the Son. The Son joyfully offers his own life and love to the Father from all eternity. This offering continues in his Incarnation. Angels sing at his birth. He can read other people's thoughts. He can raise the dead and heal the sick.

How has God blessed you? You may reflect on day 1, recalling God's love for you from the first moments of your creation. How has God continued to bless you? In your family, through your own gifts and talents, through a life of faith in the Church?

Broke. Jesus breaks the bread. There is a very practical aspect to this. He breaks the bread so that it can be shared with all of us. He reshapes this heavenly bread for his own purposes. Dramatically, the Body of Jesus is broken on the cross. His heart is literally broken, as the soldier's lance pierces it. As he hangs on the cross, following his death, the soldier's spear breaks through his Sacred Heart and out pours blood and water. St. Augustine and other writers see here an image of the sacraments of the Church flowing from the side of Jesus. Water flows out, an image of Baptism, washing us clean from sin. His Blood poured out on the cross fills the chalice at every Mass.

His heart is broken yet not destroyed. We may say that his heart is "broken open" for us as he continues to offer his love and life to us, even as his body hangs lifelessly on the cross.

Of course, it is not the Father who has "broken" Jesus. God is love. The Father offers the Son to us for our salvation in the Incarnation. In a world of sin, this gift of love is rejected, mistreated, and attacked with violence. We can see in our own sins how we have rejected God's love and turned our backs to him. Our sins and the sins of the whole world lead to this violent rejection of Emmanuel, God with us. And yet death does not have the last word. God's power shines out in the risen Christ. Jesus invites the apostle Thomas to place his hand into the wound in his heart. He says, "Bring your hand and put it into my side" (Jn 20:27). It is as if he invites Thomas to touch his Sacred Heart—pierced yet risen, beating, and alive. Jesus invites us to do the same. His heart is broken open to us, that we may offer our hearts to him and abide there eternally.

We live in a broken and wounded world. We ask ourselves, "Lord, how have I been wounded and broken?" We suffer from our own sins and the sins of others. A broken heart feels like it will never heal. The pain in that most intimate part of ourselves can limit our ability to love others and to love God. Where do we need healing? Perhaps a history of sexual sin? How have we wounded others? Or maybe you have been wounded by family members, mentors, or people in the Church?

We may not be responsible for all our wounds, but we are responsible for seeking healing. This can occur through prayer, sacraments, and conversation with family and friends. For some, it may be helpful to seek support from a spiritual director, pastor, or counselor.

Have any of your wounds helped to "break open" your heart to greater generosity and compassion? Maybe you've lost someone you love. Maybe your loss helped you support a friend during their time of mourning. I have priest friends who've dealt with alcohol addiction. Through Alcoholics Anonymous they've found sobriety and peace. Their own sobriety requires ongoing support, honesty, and humility. Flowing from this "heart wound" is a sense of understanding toward others who may be dealing with similar temptations. They are often excellent confessors, offering words of encouragement, humor, and challenge. In Christ, their broken hearts are vessels of grace for the people of God.

Gave. Jesus gives himself to the disciples in the Eucharist. This is the whole pattern of his life, of his very being. In the Incarnation, in his ministry, in the Eucharist, on the cross, Jesus gives himself to us. The Father gives Jesus to us, and Jesus joyfully accepts this mission. Mary, too, offers her son. Mary can say, too, "This is my beloved son, with whom I am well pleased."

Giving is the fun part. Giving ourselves to Christ and to others is a joy. It's not always easy, but it is worth it.

He took, blessed, broke, and gave. Let us look at the heart of Jesus as he says these words and performs these actions. He looks at us with great love at every Mass. His time with us is a time of prayer, song, ritual, nourishment, giving himself—a sacrificial offering. He concludes, "Do this in memory of me." Jesus gives himself. This is what he does. This is who he is. He gives himself to us in the Incarnation. He gives us himself in the Eucharist. Through the visions of St. Margaret Mary, he gives us his Sacred Heart. With grace we can imitate him, by giving him our hearts, too.

Questions and Exercises

1. Choose one of the revelations that Jesus spoke to St. Margaret Mary and to St. Claude. These words are given to these saints but meant for all of us. Using the Ignatian method,

allow Christ to speak to you for a few minutes "as long as the meanings, comparisons, relish, and consolations are found."

2. Choose one of the four words from the Last Supper. Go back to Matthew 26 to read his description. Reflect on this word as it applies to Jesus, to the Eucharist, and to yourself. Is there anything he wants to say to you about this word? Anything you want to say to him?

3. Look at the prayer below. It is deeply Eucharistic and closely related to the Sacred Heart. Slowly read a few lines of this prayer seeking "meanings, comparisons, relish, and consolations."

4. How does Christ abide in you?

ANIMA CHRISTI

Soul of Christ, sanctify me
Body of Christ, save me
Blood of Christ, inebriate me
Water from the side of Christ, wash me
Passion of Christ, strengthen me
O good Jesus, hear me
Within Thy wounds hide me
Permit me not to be separated from Thee
From the wicked foe defend me
In the hour of my death call me
And bid me come to Thee

That with Thy angels and saints
I may praise Thee
Forever and ever. Amen.[7]

Pause for Heart Check

You've completed six days. You're more than halfway through your retreat! Let's pause again for another quick "heart check." You could take a few minutes to do this now or you might choose to do this just before you begin day 7. Or, if you have time, you could even take a full day to review the previous chapters, look through your notes, and thank God for the graces you have received. St. Ignatius tells us that review and repetition helps us in "savoring" in our hearts the graces we receive on retreat (*SE*, 2). You may want to jot down a few notes after reflecting on these questions:

1. How is your retreat going so far?

2. Are you taking time for daily prayer?

3. Briefly read the reflections you've written in your journal.

4. What are a few highlights and graces you've received from the Lord during your retreat?

5. Are there any changes you need to make before you begin day 7?

PART III

ALL HEARTS:
ON MISSION WITH HIM

DAY 7

OFFERING MY HEART TO HIS HEART

Be missionaries already through
your prayer, by the offering of your
daily life. Your mission is here and now,
in your studies and the little things
of every day. In fulfilling it through
being open to the will of God, you are
already apostles who are helping the
entire Church.

—Fr. Francis Xavier Gautrelet, SJ, 1844[1]

The seminarian takes a deep breath.[2] He smooths out his long black cassock and runs a hand through his dark hair. He looks up at the white cross nailed over the door, makes a quick prayer as he exhales, and he knocks on the heavy dark door. It creaks slightly as he knocks and pushes it open. Fr. Francis Xavier Gautrelet, SJ, is working at his desk. On the plaster wall by his

desk hangs a small steel crucifix and a framed image of Mother
Mary, black ink on white paper. The slanting December sun
glistens on the snow as an icy chill slides over the peeling white
windowsill. He sets down his pen and turns in his chair, seeing
the young man. He takes off his glasses and smiles. "Good
morning. Come in! Are we all set for tonight?"

The young man takes a step in, more nervous now, forcing
a smile and looking at his superior, a young priest. It's Monday
afternoon, December 2, 1844. Fr. Gautrelet is friendly, smart,
faithful. He can be stern at times, especially when he's in the
middle of something. It's not easy keeping an eye on forty young
Jesuits. Many of them are devout and hardworking. A few are
immature but trying. Others are homesick or struggling with
their classes. He's around them all day, every day, and knows
them well. Each has his own habits, personality, strengths, and
temptations.

"Father, yes, I've looked over the readings for tonight. And
a few of us have been talking. We want to ask you something.
You see, we've been reading those letters that have been coming
back. And, well, we want to go, too."

"Go, too?"

Br. Henri Ramière, SJ, nods and smiles, trying to look calm
and friendly but feeling neither of these. "We've prayed about
it and talked about it. We know that we need your permission.
And we know it's not exactly the way things are usually done."

"Sit down. I'm listening. What are you hoping for?"

His lanky form strides in. He reaches for the top of a wooden chair, worn smooth by fifty years of young men grabbing it, dragging it, leaning back in it. He stands behind it, not able to sit. "We want to go now. We can be ready soon. Ready enough. They need us over there. We can help. We want to help. Christ is calling us."

He speaks about Jesuit priests in the missions. They're spread out all over the world: in South America, Asia, Eastern Europe, and Canada. French Jesuits are preaching, teaching, exploring, celebrating sacraments, building schools, setting up churches. And what are these seminarians doing? They're reading thick books in a drafty library. They're writing papers that only their teachers read, and with reluctance. In a Jesuit history course, they read excerpts from their order's heroes and saints.

St. John Brébeuf, SJ, and St. Isaac Jogues, SJ, braved shipwreck, storms, disease, snowstorms, and wild animals to bring the gospel to the native peoples of North America. Brébeuf wrote in his journal before his martyrdom, "In truth I vow to you, Jesus my Savior, that as far as I have the strength I will never fail to accept the grace of martyrdom, if some day you in your infinite mercy would offer it to me, your most unworthy servant."[3]

"I see, I see. Yes." Fr. Gautrelet looks over Henri, both smiling uneasily. Fr. Gautrelet had been inspired by St. Francis Xavier, SJ, his patron saint. Xavier was the greatest of Jesuit missionaries, a friend of St. Ignatius, and renowned throughout the Church. In the turmoil following the Reformation, Xavier's witness was a beacon of light. He voyaged to Asia, learned languages, performed miracles, risked his life, baptized thousands. Fr. Gautrelet had read Xavier's urgent letters to Ignatius from the missions: "There is no one to say Mass, no one to teach them the creed . . . I have often felt strongly moved to go to the universities of Europe, especially Paris, crying out like a madman, and say to those in the Sorbonne who have more learning than goodwill to employ it advantageously: 'How many souls are missing heaven and going to hell through your negligence?'"[4] These words have enflamed the hearts of Jesuits for centuries. These young men wanted to be like Xavier, as their superiors had urged them to do. Fr. Gautrelet looked down and then closed his eyes.

After ordination, Fr. Gautrelet settled into leadership roles in the Jesuit order in France. Young Jesuits need guidance, food, learning, and support. He knew all this. He also read the newspapers and kept up with Jesuit friends in Paris: social unrest, protests in the streets, violence, and secularism—especially among the young. Was this the new normal? The French Revolution continued to reverberate. Napoleon's conquest of France and then Europe, followed by his defeat and demise; now with "enlightened," secular, wealthy men running the press and the government, with the Church mocked or simply ignored. In 1844, a Catholic king was on the throne again; he'd be overthrown four years later. The Jesuits talked about it. Everyone talked about it. What did it all mean? What could they do? How should the Church respond?

Things were quieter in Vals, in southern France, and in the other small towns. Change started in Paris but would all come here eventually. Fr. Gautrelet recalled feeling the same urgency that Ramière expressed: "We've got to do something!" Fr. Gautrelet's generation of Jesuits had stayed the course, channeled their energy into prayer and service—teaching, preaching, serving the poor.

Fr. Gautrelet had asked to go to the missions. His superiors said, "We need you here." It was an odd sacrifice, not going to the missions. He labored in French parishes, Church administration, celebrating Mass, preaching to seminarians. His assignments were all were received in obedience. Later, his request was granted and he was sent to Algiers, Africa, for an assignment.[5] What about the next generation? How to inspire these young men while urging patience as they prepared for the priesthood? "Read Aquinas now and be a missionary later." It was a hard sell sometimes, especially with the latest headlines.

Henri spoke again and Fr. Gautrelet opened his eyes. "Father, I prayed about it last night. Maybe we're not fully ready. But they weren't ready either. It's just like you said. Was St. John ready? Did Peter have a theology degree? God chooses the weak to humble the strong." Beads of sweat emerged at his hairline. His palms were damp and he felt hot under the black wool robe. Would the old man go for it? Maybe. He'd need to recount this conversation to his friends after dinner. "What did he say?" they'd ask. "Well, I said . . . and then he said . . . and I told him . . ." He needed to show that he'd done his best and presented their argument convincingly. Some missionaries were called by God. Sometimes they volunteered themselves. Xavier wasn't even Ignatius's first choice. Another man backed out at the last minute. Xavier said, "Let me get my coat and prayer book and then I'll be on the ship."

Fr. Gautrelet smiled. The priest folded his glasses and cleared his throat. "Brother, these are holy desires to be sure. But you know the plan for our formation. I did it myself. After novitiate, three years of philosophy studies, beginning with the ancients. Then . . ."

"We want to be like the apostles," Henri blurted.

"Like the apostles," said the priest. "Like the apostles." He nodded. "Tell you what. I've got a meeting in a few minutes. Let me give it some thought. Can we talk tomorrow after lunch?"

"Yes. Thank you, Father. And happy feast—well, the eve of the feast!" He nodded and left. He would pray, wait, talk to the guys, and see what Fr. Gautrelet would say tomorrow.

Tomorrow was December 3, 1844, the Feast of St. Francis Xavier. They would start early with a festive Mass, with songs, candles, and a procession. Xavier studied in Paris where he was a roommate of Ignatius. Ignatius was beloved by his Jesuit sons, but his story is more opaque for the average Catholic: "So Ignatius wrote a book and was a church administrator. That's it?" Xavier's glory was obvious.

Fr. Gautrelet had been thinking and praying about this homily for weeks. Henri's blunt request underlined the urgency of the situation. Would they mutiny? Unlikely. But there's a big difference between seminarians eagerly pursuing their prayers and studies—and young men glumly biding their time. "We're ready now." Maybe he could say something tonight at evening prayer. Typically this was a brief sermon, with the longer one in the morning. Maybe he needed to "go big" tonight to grab their attention and respond to their request now.

They filed into the candlelit chapel that evening. He began in the usual way, a brief summary of the scripture passage they'd just heard. Then a word on the disciples of Jesus and how the great Jesuits continue this spirit of faith and service as disciples and apostles, servants and pastors, missionaries, and friends. A standard opening. He continued, "If each one infuses his labors with the spirit of prayer and makes of them an offering; if several jointly direct themselves in the same way, there would be a convergence of power capable of lifting up mountains!" He picked up the pace, got louder, looked at each of them, and slid his notes to the side. The words flowed. His prayer had been answered: "Lord, speak from your heart, through my heart, to their hearts."

"Be missionaries already through your prayer, by the offering of your daily life. Your mission is here and now, in your studies and the little things of every day. In fulfilling it through being open to the will of God, you are already apostles who are helping the entire Church. Pray for the people you will meet tomorrow."[6]

He could hear his own heart beating. A drop of salty sweat dripped from his hairline to the corner of his mouth. A hundred eyes looked at his. He saw Henri's dark eyes smiling. The young man wasn't restless but resolved. "Missionaries already." "Offering your daily life." Fr. Gautrelet stepped away from the podium, bowed to the altar, and sat down. He and Henri both heard fifty hearts beating.

That night in 1844, the Apostleship of Prayer was born. It was so simple: offering our lives to Christ each day. Uniting our hearts with his Sacred Heart for the salvation of all hearts. A mustard seed on the Feast of St. Francis Xavier took root in the hearts of fifty young Jesuits. This little movement spread around the nation, the continent, and the world. In two years, it was blessed by the local bishop. A few years later, Pope Pius IX officially recognized the group and offered indulgences to anyone who made a morning offering to the Sacred Heart. Henri Ramière, SJ, was soon ordained; in 1861 he wrote the statutes for the fledgling group. All Christians could be apostles through prayer, united in the King of apostles. We offer our lives along with him. This was the continuation and fulfillment of St. Margaret Mary's visions two hundred years earlier. Her personal encounter with the heart of Jesus could now be shared by millions. Further, this offering was infused with a spirit of mission rooted in the heart of the Church. Private visions became shared, public devotion. It was now a movement, infused with a spirit of evangelization and re-evangelization. In 1890 Pope Leo XIII began writing monthly prayer intentions to be promoted by the Apostleship. In 1899, he consecrated the world to the Sacred Heart. In time, the movement included retreats, prayer groups, magazines, art, poetry, musicals, and youth branches. In the United States, Jesuits preached about it on the radio and TV, in traveling mission bands, and through sodalities (prayer groups at Jesuit schools and parishes). As Ramière writes, Christ himself "consecrated the first thirty years of his mortal life exclusively to the Apostleship of Prayer."[7] This was the first mission of Jesus: prayer. In his first thirty years, known as the "hidden life," he spent time at home with Mary and Joseph. He studied the Torah, the prophets, and the Jewish scriptures. He worked in Joseph's carpentry shop. If Christ lived this way, shouldn't we? He is the beating heart at the center of this spunky band. He wants to draw hearts to himself, set them on fire, and send them out to the world in his mission: the salvation of all hearts.

OVERVIEW OF THE DAY FROM IGNATIUS: WE RECEIVE SO THAT WE MAY GIVE

In offering myself to Christ and offering my heart to his Sacred Heart, my response is simply a response to his offering to me. At every Mass, Christ says to me, "Take this all of you, this is my Body." I ask to receive his gift with faith and love. I then respond each day with my own humble offering: "O Jesus, I offer you myself, for your great mission of salvation." St. Ignatius begins his famous prayer, "Take, Lord, receive, all my liberty."

My offering flows from a deep sense of gratitude to the Lord. Ignatius writes, "I will call back into my memory the gifts I

have received—my creation, redemption, and other gifts particular to myself. I will ponder with deep affection how much God
our Lord has done for me, and how much he has given me of
what he possesses, and consequently how he, the same Lord,
desires to give me even his very self" (*SE*, 234). Pondering and
ruminating on God's many gifts, I consider my own response.
Do I just say a quick thanks and go on my way? Or should I
make some effort to reciprocate? I'm immediately struck by
God's immensity and my weakness. The Father gives me his
Son and I offer him a few hours of work and leisure today? Like
the poor widow, I can offer my little coins. I offer to God what
I have: myself.

God asks us to do nothing that he has not already done for
us. Let's take a moment to recall and review the graces from
the first day of our current retreat. "In the beginning, there was
love." St. John, the beloved disciple says it this way: "We love
because he first loved us" (1 Jn 4:19). Recall our contemplation
of God shaping and forming us in our mothers' wombs. Our
parents prayed for us and loved us even before we could see or
speak. God handcrafts us, shaping us according to his image
and likeness from the first moment of our conception. Further,
Christ gives himself to us in the Incarnation and the Eucharist,
and upon the cross.

"I will ask for interior knowledge of all
the great good I have received, in order
that, stirred to profound gratitude, I may
become able to love and serve the Divine
Majesty in all things" (*SE*, 233).

CONTEMPLATION:
OFFERING MY HEART

Using the method of St. Ignatius, we will slowly pray through the traditional Daily Offering prayer of the Pope's Worldwide Prayer Network,[8] which is the Apostleship of Prayer. In the questions at the end of this day, I'll encourage you to pray with St. Ignatius's Suscipe prayer, too (see day 9). This reflection will be in the first person, using "I"—and I hope this helps you to pray it, too. Here's the Daily Offering:

> O Jesus, through the Immaculate Heart of Mary,
> I offer You my prayers, works, joys, and sufferings of this day
> in union with the Holy Sacrifice of the Mass throughout the world.
> I offer them for all the intentions of Your Sacred Heart:
> the salvation of souls, reparation for sin,
> and the reunion of all Christians.
> I offer them for the intentions of our bishops

> and of all Apostles of Prayer,
> and in particular for those recommended
> by our Holy Father this month.
> Amen.[9]

The genius of Fr. Gautrelet was in crafting a simple prayer to offer our hearts to the Sacred Heart every day. "O Jesus, through the Immaculate Heart of Mary, I offer . . . " In essence, I offer everything to the Lord. I offer myself as Jesus offers himself to me. I receive him and trust that he will receive me. I do this with Mother Mary. She first felt your divine heart beating beneath her heart. She was a spiritual mother to the early disciples, and she walks with me now.

Clearly it is not easy to make a wholehearted offering of ourselves to Jesus every day. Sin, temptation, laziness, worldliness, and selfishness can all get in the way. The subtle temptation is to be content with a halfhearted offering. Pope Francis tried to stir us from this comfortable slumber when he said:

> God came out of himself to come among us,
> he pitched his tent among us to bring to us his
> mercy that saves and gives hope. Nor must we
> be satisfied with staying in the pen of the 99
> sheep if we want to follow him and to remain
> with him; we too must 'go out' with him to
> seek the lost sheep, the one that has strayed
> the furthest. Be sure to remember: coming out
> of ourselves, just as Jesus, just as God came
> out of himself in Jesus and Jesus came out of
> himself for all of us. Someone might say to

> me: "but Father, I don't have time." "I have so
> many things to do," "it's difficult." "what can
> I do with my feebleness and my sins, with so
> many things?"[10]

To these questions and doubts, Jesus responds, "Behold the Heart." As I behold his heart, I'm move with a desire to offer my heart to His Heart for all hearts. This is the mystery of the Sacred Heart devotion. This is the mystery of Christian life. God wants to be with us. He wants us. He is Emmanuel, *God with us*. The Son of God becomes the son of Mary.

I make my offering from my heart, through his heart, for all hearts. This is a personal offering to the heart of Jesus who made me and loves me. "I offer me to you, Lord . . ." For me, this prayer is one of the few things I do before my morning coffee each day. No matter what happens, no matter how this day turns out: "Lord, I want to begin my day united with you." A classic Jesuit slogan for this prayer is "Fifteen seconds to start the day right!" Or, more succinctly, "It starts the day right."

"Through the Immaculate Heart of Mary." At the start of this prayer, we also see that we're not alone. Mary, the mother of Jesus, is always with her son. Thus, if we are with him, we're with her, too. We unite our hearts with her heart and with the heart of Jesus.

I offer my "prayers, works, joys, and sufferings." This is a brief yet comprehensive summary of what is ahead for me today. The next sixteen hours will have all of these. I'm beginning my day with prayer. After coffee and breakfast (and more coffee)

I'll move into work. For some, this is manual labor; for others
it is office work, teaching, health care, study, childcare, or even
a quiet day of rest. It might go well today—with success, appre-
ciation, and satisfaction. It might be the opposite. I don't have
full control over the outcome. I can only offer it all to Christ
and ask to do my best.

"Joys and sufferings": Both will come, but not in equal
measure. Jesus experienced both joy and sorrow in his ministry. I will, too. Here, too, I do not have full control over the
results. I can seek to live with a spirit of openness, hope, and
service toward Christ and others. I wish to mingle my joys and
sufferings with the joys and suffering of Jesus.

"In union with the holy sacrifice of the Mass throughout
the world": I'm now reminded of the sixth day, "Christ abides in
us." At Mass, the priest invites us to "lift up our hearts" and we
"lift them up to the Lord." As a priest, I'm blessed to celebrate
Mass each day. The Church and the people of God ask this of
me, expect it, and rejoice in it. Some lay Catholics are able to
attend daily Mass, or perhaps Mass every Friday. For others, this
is not possible. Whether we attend daily or weekly, the Mass
is offered for us and for the world. We are part of a universal,
global communion in the Body of Christ, the Church. Imagine
the sun rising in each country, in each time zone, and priests
in every city offering Mass before the faithful—sometimes
thousands in a cathedral, sometimes a dozen in a little village
church. As the sun sets, another wave of evening Masses greets
the moonlight, from sea to shining sea. As we offer our hearts

to the Sacred Heart of Jesus, we're drawn more deeply into the Body of Christ, the Church. Truly his heart is the beating center of the Church, sending out his life and love to every hand and foot, every eye and ear, every child and woman and man around the world.

"For all the intentions of your Sacred Heart": He plunges me into the life of the Church. Christ wants every soul to be saved, every sin forgiven, every Christian united in him. I'm drawn into the contemporary challenges facing the Church and the world. Each month, the pope offers a special prayer intention that is entrusted to his prayer network, the Apostleship of Prayer. These range from the dramatic to the timeless to the unexpected. In recent years, we've prayed for families, migrants, care for the environment, women, those who work at sea, and the ethical use of robots and artificial intelligence. Christ's mission continues as he sails in Peter's boat over the rolling waves of human history.

Jesus touches my heart. He unites my heart with his Sacred Heart. I am not alone. I'm part of a worldwide community of disciples, serving his mission through prayer and action. Through him and in the Church, I can touch all hearts in my love and prayer.

Questions and Exercises

1. What are some of the gifts in your life? Which of these gifts is easiest for you to offer to the Lord?

2. Which of these gifts is hardest for you to offer to the Lord?

3. Drawing on the visions of St. Margaret Mary, prayerfully imagine offering your heart to Jesus. What does your heart look like? What are some of the blessings in your heart? What are the wounds and scars?

4. Henri Ramière, SJ, wanted to be like the apostles and great missionaries. Ask Christ how he is calling you to be a missionary (in ways big and small).

5. How does Jesus respond as he receives your heart? Is there anything you wish to say to him? Anything he wants to say to you? Anything you want him to do with your heart (blessing, healing, etc.)?

CENTER OF OUR HEARTS

O God, what will you do to conquer
the fearful hardness of our hearts?
Lord, you must give us new hearts,
to replace hearts that are made of marble and of bronze.
You must give us your own Heart, Jesus.
Come, lovable Heart of Jesus.
Place your Heart deep in the center of our hearts
and enkindle in each heart a flame of love
as strong, as great, as the sum of all the reasons
that I have for loving You, my God.
O holy Heart of Jesus, dwell in my heart,

So that I may live only in you and for you,
So that, in the end, I may live with you eternally in
    Heaven. Amen.
        —St. Claude de La Colombière, SJ (1641–1682,
            known as the Apostle of the Sacred Heart)[11]

THE HEART OF THE MISSION

Consider how the Lord of all the world chooses so many persons, apostles, disciples, and the like. He sends them throughout the whole world, to spread his doctrine among people of every state.
—*Spiritual Exercises*, 144

I'm pouring sweat. I stand a foot taller than anyone else. The chapel is the size of a two-car garage, filled with mourners. It's dark and hot, humid and still. The village elder swings a clay thurible from a black iron chain. Fragrant incense pours out, seasoned with local herbs. Everyone is singing a hymn in Mayan. A few beams of sunlight break through the open windows, cutting through the smoke. It's hard to see and hard to breathe. A man's wife has died. He is reaching into the wooden coffin, gently sliding the wedding ring off her hand. He is praying,

weeping, and speaking to her in Mayan. Two men bring up
the wooden lid and place it on top of the casket. Another man
walks up with a fistful of nails and a large mallet. He pounds the
nails into the lid. *Tink, tink.* The steel hammer hits the steel nail,
pounding it in; and then a *thunk* as the hammer hits the wooden
lid, sealing the coffin. The chants grow louder. Children kick a
red ball near the door. Many of them wear donated American
T-shirts: Nike, Dallas Cowboys, Miami Beach. The men wear
white button shirts and dark khakis with thick leather belts.
The women wear richly woven blouses, their Sunday best, with
embroidered birds and flowers in a scoop around the neck. A
chicken and a dog stare at each other in the sun by the entrance.
Suddenly, an older woman's cell phone buzzes, and we hear a
Beyoncé ringtone: "All the single ladies, all the single ladies, all
the single ladies!" She answers it in Mayan. She says curtly, I
think, "I'm in church. I'll call you later. Bye."

I was assigned to a Mayan parish in Belize, Central America, shortly after my ordination. Midwestern Jesuits have served
there for over a hundred years. I was honored, excited, and a
little nervous. I'd read about our Jesuit missionaries in past
centuries, including St. Francis Xavier and St. John Brébeuf.
I admired their bravery, creativity, and generosity. For a few
months, in my own small way, I'd be a part of this great tradition.

Belize is a former British colony. It's been independent since
only 1981. It's the size of Massachusetts, less than a million
people, with varied geography, cultures, and languages. The
sparkling Caribbean Sea and white beaches draw tourists and

locals. Rain forests, low mountains, and wildlife fill the steaming central corridor. Sip coffee under an umbrella at a sidewalk cafe in the capital city and you'll hear Belizeans speaking Spanish, English, Mayan, and Creole—sometimes in the same conversation.

My job was to drive out to rural villages in the southern part of the country. Many of these villages have Mass only every four to eight weeks. Mayans have lived in Central America for thousands of years. Most of them are now Christians, amid their own language, culture, and traditions. Here the postmodern world collides with an ancient heritage. Subsistence farming, ancient rituals, Nikes, and cell phones exist side by side.

One Saturday evening, I was set to drive out to one of the far-out villages, near the Guatemala border. It would be a solid two-hour drive. I ate a quick dinner and left before sunset. Ideally, I'd get there shortly after the villagers had their own dinner, following a hot day in their fields. I'd offer Mass, baptize several babies, and hear Confession in the morning. Then I'd drive back, stopping for two more Masses along the way. A young Jesuit novice, JP, was riding with me. He was on a short ministry "experiment" with me. He helped with Confirmation preparation at village schools and chapels. He'd be my sidekick and acolyte.

Earlier in the day, the older Jesuit pastor, Fr. Mo (Maurice) had drawn me a map on the back of a dinner napkin. He knew this country like the back of his hand, spending decades here as a teacher, priest, and pastor. He drew a long snaky line to indicate the main road. He made an *X*: "There used to be a gas station here, but it burned down. Turn left there." How would I know where a gas station used to be? "There's a river here. The bridge might be out. It depends how much rain they've had. Did you bring boots?" Yes. "Be sure you take them off because the water will be over your knees." I shot a few glances at JP during this instruction; he smiled back. "Ok, Mo. Anything else?" "You'll be fine. Bring some water and snacks. They'll be waiting for you."

We hopped in the white Toyota 4 x 4. It had *at least* four hundred thousand miles on it; the odometer was broken and no longer registered miles. Four hundred thousand miles: that's sixteen times around the equator, and it looked like it. Calling it white is also an overstatement. I could look through the rusty fender and see the engine rattling. I had never driven a stick shift before I came to Belize. Now I could do it, though not well.

We were off. The sun sets in Central America at 6:00 p.m. every day. This was during the rainy season, which runs from January to December. Last night was a big storm. There were puddles in the valleys. The two-lane road was paved for the first few miles. Then gravel, then dirt, then mud. After a few months in Belize, I had a basic sense of the driving style. Step on the gas when going downhill so that you could splash through the big puddles in the valleys. Then keep your foot on the gas going uphill so you don't kill the engine. Gas and more gas. The windshield wipers stopped working during Ronald Reagan's second term. I had a handkerchief with me and a water bottle. I would douse the windshield with water and then reach out and wipe off the mud. Sometimes I had to do this to clean mud off the inside of the windshield—that's right, *inside* of the windshield. The sun was almost down. JP and I talked. It was loud and bouncy.

At the bottom of a big hill, I slid through a mud puddle and then felt an ugly bump rattle up my spinal cord: a big rock, at fifty miles per hour. Next was a big flash from under the hood and a thud. I hit the gas and nothing happened. The truck rolled to a stop as smoke oozed from the hood. We got out. Twenty feet behind the truck, the battery was on the ground, smoldering. "JP, you know anything about cars?" No. "Me neither. I guess we walk."

The last glimmers of sunlight slid behind the green horizon. We grabbed our bags, the dinner-napkin map, and walked. It was almost dark, then pitch black. We could barely see the road six feet from our eyes. We talked, prayed a Rosary, and laughed. Would we get lost or attacked by a jaguar? He stopped. "Hey, Father, look up." A hundred billion stars shone out. We could see every one. I saw the constellations: the Big Dipper and Orion's Belt. A full moon peeked over the horizon. As it rose, it lit up the road. We could see. Howler monkeys squawked from the trees.

We were sweaty and exhausted. We had no camping gear. Up ahead, I saw a man-shaped shadow. The moonlight flashed off the machete near his belt. "*Padre. Padrecito?*" Priest, Father?

"Yes?" I replied.

"*Conmigo.*" Come with me, he said.

The villagers sent the young guide to find us. We walked behind him on the road and then turned down a footpath into the forest. We walked up a hill and into a clearing to the village. Little houses and huts, pastures, a few dogs wandering around. In the center, the outline of a chapel with light glowing within. We walked in. Three tall candles burned before the wooden altar. The whole village was singing and praying, waiting for us.

English is their third language. Mayan is first, Spanish is second. I speak a little Spanish. "*Hola, hola. Gracias, gracias,*" I said, waving. The village elder walked up to us. A dark-haired stocky man, maybe sixty years old, in a white shirt. A younger man stood next to him, translating from Mayan to Spanish. "Father, we've been waiting for you. We've been praying for you. We knew you would come, that God would bring you here." I had that dazed feeling that comes from physical and mental exhaustion. I could feel myself rocking back and forth slightly. "Yes, thank you. I'm so sorry. We had a problem with our truck so we had to walk." "Yes, Father. We have some water for you to drink and to wash your face. Then you will say Mass. We have been waiting for you. For three hours." He smiled. I was dazed with exhaustion. The babies were dressed in white baptismal gowns, sleeping. They were ready now. I looked at JP. "Wash your face. I'll set up for Mass," he said.

There in the darkness, on top of the mountain (okay, a hill), in a village chapel, I celebrated Mass. This is why I came and why they waited. This is the source and summit of Christian life. The Body of Christ is the fountain and source from which all graces flow. The Eucharist is the summit, the mountaintop, where our pathway leads. Renewed by this bread from heaven, he sends us back down the mountain into the nitty-gritty love and labor of daily life.

In the sacraments, in the Church, and in prayer God comes to us. He supported me and my Jesuit brother; together we talked, laughed and prayed. God lights our path through the stars and moonlight. God blessed us in the prayers of the villagers, with his light shining in three candles. Most powerfully, he comes to us in the Mass. Christ draws us to himself, feeding us with his Body and Blood. He then sends us out on mission. "Do this in memory of me," and "Go forth, the Mass is ended." Christian faith is not simply about believing in the truth. It is about putting our faith in action: Do. Go.

OVERVIEW OF THE DAY FROM IGNATIUS: ON A MISSION WITH JESUS

My time in Belize was an experience of being on mission with Jesus. He calls us to labor with him, in ways big and small. In this meditation, you'll consider your own call to serve Christ and his people. Let's reflect on Christ the King. St. Ignatius invites us to imagine Jesus speaking to all of us. Jesus says, "My will is to conquer the whole world and all my enemies, and thus to enter into the glory of my Father. Therefore, whoever wishes to come with me must labor with me, so that through following me in the pain he may follow me also in the glory" (*SE*, 95).

Let's take a moment to reflect on ourselves. How is Christ calling us? How can we share in his great mission of salvation? St. Ignatius draws us in further: "Consider how the Lord of all the world chooses so many persons, apostles, disciples, and the like. He sends them throughout the whole world, to spread his doctrine among people of every state" (*SE*, 145). In Belize, I saw that I stood in a long line of Jesuit missionaries, pastors, and teachers. Through those first preachers, the Holy Spirit had drawn the Belizean people into the life of Christ. They were sharing the faith with their children and grandchildren through their schools, catechists, and family prayer. In my own family, Christ had worked through generations of priests, teachers, and missionaries to reach me through my ancestors in Germany, France, and Italy. In the small town of Nazareth, God became man; there, Mary says yes to the angel, and the child Jesus is conceived in her womb. Like Belize, Nazareth was a forgotten corner of a global empire. In Nazareth, Jesus grew from an infant to a boy to a young man. Through his preaching, ministry, and disciples, faith in Christ spread in Israel through the Roman Empire and beyond.

Now, we too pray for the grace to consider how Christ calls us. He desires that all of his followers come to labor with him for his kingdom. I ask that he may receive me in his mission in the world today (*SE*, 137). Ignatius, like a good spiritual director, helps us to make this offering and suggests the following formula: address God, identify your offering, name the saints who have helped you make this offering, and conclude with your desire to align yourself with God's will (see *SE*, 98).

"That I may not be deaf to his call, but
ready and diligent to accomplish his most
holy will" (*SE*, 91).

CONTEMPLATION:
ON THE BATTLEFIELD WITH MY KING

One of Pope Francis's favorite gospel passages is the good Samaritan. He frequently highlighted it in the Jubilee Year of Mercy in 2015–16. He used it in the logo for the jubilee. It is the centerpiece of his encyclical *Fratelli Tutti*, as well as an apt image for his description of the Church as a field hospital. He certainly has this passage in mind when he speaks of his dream of a "Church of mercy." It is one of the most famous stories in the Bible, familiar to Christians and unbelievers alike. Let's begin at the end. After telling the parable, Jesus asks, "Which of these three, in your opinion, was neighbor?" The man answered, "The one who treated him with mercy." Jesus said to him, "Go and do likewise" (Lk 10:36–37). Jesus affirms the man and then sends him out: "Go. Do." He sends him on a mission of compassion. He sends us, too, on the same mission of mercy.

Jesus is our king. He is the Father's true missionary, and the whole world is his mission field. Let's again use our imaginations as we contemplate his call for us. We place ourselves before Christ the King as he says to us, "My will is to conquer the whole world . . . Therefore, whoever wishes to come with me must labor with me." You might imagine Christ as a great king, as in some religious artwork. Or perhaps he comes to you as a shepherd or teacher.

First, ask, "What have I done for Christ?" (*SE*, 53). If you are reading this book and making time for prayer, probably you have been following Christ for several years. You may be quick to add, "But I'm doing it imperfectly! I still have a long way to go!" That's true for me, too. We've gotten this far, so we must be doing something right. Tell the Lord a few things you have done for him. These activities are a form of praise, as he is the one who has given us the grace to do all of this for him. Also recall some of the gifts that he has given you: the grace of Baptism, in hearing the gospel message, in knowing Jesus as a Savior and friend. His grace is at work in us and he has great plans for us.

Second, ask, "What am I doing for you, Lord?" In the gospels, the mission of his disciples is wide ranging. "He summoned the Twelve and began to send them out two by two and gave them authority over unclean spirits. He instructed them to take nothing for the journey but a walking stick—no food, no sack, no money in their belts. . . . So they went off and preached repentance. They drove out many demons, and they anointed with oil many who were sick and cured them" (Mk 6:7–8, 12–13). They are teaching, healing, serving, and loving. They imitate Jesus in his great mission of compassion. With Jesus, the whole world is our mission field. This includes faraway lands, our cities, neighborhoods, and kitchen tables.

I ask, "What am I doing for him now? What is my vocation now? Lord, what am I doing for you? And just as importantly, how am I doing it? In what areas do I labor with generosity and love? And where am I shirking my call? Where am I burying my treasure—wasting too much time scrolling through social media and binge-watching TV?"

Third, ask, "What will I do for you, Lord?" Is there something new Christ is calling you to? Or is he calling you to do something familiar in a new way? Perhaps a waiter is called to share his faith more openly with colleagues in the kitchen. Maybe a mother desires to bring her kids to visit a nursing home each month. Some image may grab your heart right now: "Lord, I think you are calling me to this place: _____." His mission of compassion reaches to the ends of the earth. Jesus tells us, "As the Father has sent me, so I send you" (Jn 20:21). We are the hands and feet of the Body of Christ, with his heart giving us strength to do his will.

Here, I may want to start small. "Lord, what are a few small ways that I can love and serve you more?" This could mean attending one additional Mass each week, or more faithfulness to my daily prayer. Or maybe he's calling me to go big: "Lord, are you calling me to a heroic mission? To Belize, to the unchurched, to the poorest in my own city?" I want to offer myself as generously as possible. Look at the Bible: he calls ordinary people to do extraordinary things. Jesus even becomes an ordinary person: "Is he not the carpenter's son?" (Mt 13:55). And he does extraordinary things in us.

He may call me to be a small part of something big or a big part of something small. Belize needs teachers, pastors, business leaders, and benefactors; one person's role may be small but could have a big impact. Families need parents, grandparents, babysitters, and youth ministers. Christ may call you to do something small and beautiful for one family: your neighbor's or your own.

Jesus draws us to himself in friendship and service. It is not an obligation, but an invitation from our eternal King. What could be better, more glorious, and more meaningful than joining him in his grand mission of salvation? He loves you and invites you as he invited Mary and Peter and Ignatius and so many others through the centuries. He has a unique call for you in this great mission of salvation. Your response can be the same as those great saints: "Yes," "Fiat," "Amen!"

Questions and Exercises

1. Imagine yourself before Christ the King. Speak with him about those three questions, above: "What have I done for you? What am I doing for you? What will I do for you?" Is there anything he wants to say to you? Jot down a few notes in your journal.

2. Is there one small thing Christ is calling you to now? A phone call to an elderly relative? Going to Confession (especially if it has been a while)?

3. Is there one big thing Christ is calling you to do—even if your role in it may be small? A donation to a Catholic charity?

4. Each month, the pope offers a special intention, asking the whole Church to pray and work together in a "mission of compassion." In recent years, this list has included migrants, women, and those who work at sea. Find the list here: popesprayerusa.net/popes-intentions/. Choose one intention from this year and pray for it. Then do a quick internet search to learn more about it. Is there something small that you can do to help? Volunteering, donating, advocating?

5. Pray the prayer below. Ask Christ how he can use you as a channel of his peace. Pray for the grace to "consider how Christ calls and desires all persons to come under his standard" (*SE*, 137).

PRAYER OF ST. FRANCIS

Make me a channel of your peace
Where there is hatred let me bring your love
Where there is injury, your pardon Lord
And where there is doubt true faith in You
Make me a channel of your peace
Where there is despair in life let me bring hope
Where there is darkness only light
And where there's sadness ever joy
Oh, Master, grant that I may never seek
So much to be consoled as to console
To be understood as to understand
To be loved as to love with all my soul

Make me a channel of your peace
It is in pardoning that we are pardoned
It is in giving to all that we receive
And in dying that we are born to eternal life.[1]

UNITED WITH CHRIST, LOVING AND SERVING ALL HEARTS

We are called to be witnesses and messengers of God's mercy, to offer the world a perspective of light where darkness is, of hope where despair reigns, of salvation where sin abounds. To enter into prayer is to enter with my heart into the heart of Jesus.

—Pope Francis, on the 175th anniversary of the Apostleship of Prayer[1]

Catholic tongue twister—ready? The Body of Christ gives the Body of Christ to the Body of Christ, so the Body of Christ becomes more like the Body of Christ to serve the Body of Christ. Got it? Read it again.

Translation: Jesus gives the Eucharist to the Church to make us more like him so that we can serve him in others. The New Testament speaks of the Body of Christ in many ways. Jesus is the Body of Christ. The Eucharist is the Body of Christ. We, the Church, are the Body of Christ. In a special way, Jesus identifies the poor with himself as he tells us, "Whatever you did for one of the least of my brothers of mine, you did for me" (Mt 25:40). We are made in the image and likeness of his Body. We are wounded by sin, and Christ draws us to his heart. He renews and strengthens us. He feeds us with his Body and Blood and sends us out on mission to serve his Body in the world.

Look at the saints: young and old, male and female, rich and poor, brilliant and simple, priests and nuns, mothers and fathers, children and martyrs; some traveled thousands of miles to faraway lands, and some stayed in their hometowns. They are not "cookie cutters," all identical. We're all called to holiness in Christ, but the pathway is different for each of us. His grace purifies and perfects us, shaping us into true sons and daughters of the Father. All saints are united in his heart and in his mission. He wants to make our hearts more like his Sacred Heart so that he can touch hearts through us.

On this final day of retreat, let's ask, "Where do we go from here?" First let's review where we've been and then we can see where to go next. On day 1, we began by reflecting on God's goodness: "In the beginning there was love." The divine Trinity lives in eternal loving relationship; God created our hearts in love in our mothers' wombs. On day 2 we considered our own hearts, "restless and needy." We are made for relationship with God and others. We looked at the call of St. Ignatius and the need for "discernment of spirits" as both the Holy Spirit and the evil spirit are at work in the world. On day 3 we confronted the brokenness of our world around us. Sin, violence, death, and confusion are daily encounters. On this battlefield, the bright flag of Christ snaps crisply in the wind, calling us to humility, love, and service. The dark flag of Satan tempts us with empty riches, honors, and pride.

On day 4 we contemplated the Incarnation. Like children trapped in a dark maze, we cannot free ourselves. The Father sends his Son to save us. Conceived and born of Mary, God has a living, beating human heart for the first time in history. On day 5 we see that "he calls us his friends." Jesus calls us as disciples and friends. In a heart-to-heart relationship, Christ wants us to know him and to make ourselves known to him. On day 6 we focused on the visions of the Sacred Heart given to St. Margaret Mary Alacoque. In the Eucharist, "Christ abides in us" as he feeds us with his own Body and Blood.

On day 7, at his invitation, we offer our lives along with him for the salvation of all hearts. Receiving his heart, we now offer ours to him for the salvation of all hearts. We explored the beginnings of the Apostleship of Prayer with Fr. Gautrelet, SJ, and Henri Ramière, SJ, in France in the 1840s. Together with the whole Church, we can offer our hearts to the Sacred Heart of Jesus each day. On day 8 we explored Christ's mission of compassion over the whole face of the earth. In ways big and small, we are called to daily love and to serve him and his people.

That's where we've been. So where do we go from here? I've been on many retreats in my Jesuit life. Jesuits are expected to make a retreat each summer. Frequently I've been assigned to Jesuit schools. After nine months of teaching, leading retreats, and supervising field trips, I'm usually ready for quiet and reflection (and a long nap). At the end of a good retreat, I feel refreshed and renewed. I've had time to reflect on my life, on the ways God has been at work in my heart, and on the moments when I've turned away from his call. And at the end of a good retreat, I'm often asking, "Now what, Lord?" Newfound zeal for Christ and his kingdom can be invigorating and disorienting. Should I start a new club at my school? Should I work on my Spanish? Or maybe I should ask my superior if I can serve at a homeless shelter in my spare time?

From another angle, I can also feel overwhelmed by the needs in the world around me: poverty, faithlessness, and indifference. I ask, "Lord, what can I do? Will my small effort make a difference?"

In a Lenten message, Pope Francis wrote:

> As individuals too, we are tempted by indifference. Flooded with news reports and troubling images of human suffering, we often feel our complete inability to help. What can we do to

> avoid being caught up in this spiral of distress
> and powerlessness?
>
> First, we can pray in communion with
> the Church on earth and in heaven. Let us not
> underestimate the power of so many voices
> united in prayer![2]

Love and service. Prayer and work, *ora et labora*, in the words of St. Benedict. We, too, "want to be like the apostles," as Henri Ramière, SJ, blurted to his superior almost two hundred years ago. More deeply, we want to be like the first apostle: Jesus. He is the true missionary sent by the Father to announce the Good News of his salvation to the whole world. Earlier we considered the life of St. Francis Xavier, SJ. He was obviously a hero and a true apostle, traveling to the farthest lands to preach the name of Jesus. As the Apostleship of Prayer was born on his feast day, he is the group's first patron saint. And the Apostleship has another patron saint. A young girl felt a similar desire to imitate Jesus. She was Thérèse Martin, the most famous member of the Apostleship of Prayer. You know her as St. Thérèse of Lisieux. She is the youngest Doctor of the Church, and one of four women to receive this title.

Her membership card is on file at our archives in Rome.[3] She joined shortly before her thirteenth birthday in 1885. She began each day by offering her heart to the Sacred Heart of Jesus for the salvation of all hearts—especially for the monthly prayer intention of the Holy Father. In her autobiography, she would later write, "O Jesus, my Love . . . my Love . . . my vocation, at last I have found it. . . . MY VOCATION IS LOVE. Yes, I have found my place in the Church and it is You, O my God, who have given me this place; in the heart of the Church, my Mother, I shall be *Love*."[4] Her home is in the Sacred Heart, in the center of the Church. She would also write, in a mystical vision, "O my Beloved, one mission alone would not be sufficient for me, I would want to preach the Gospel on all the five continents simultaneously and even to the most remote isles. I would be a missionary, not for a few years only but from the beginning of creation until the consummation [end] of the ages. But above all, O my Beloved Savior, I would shed my blood for You even to the very last drop."[5] She wants to be like the martyrs, like the apostles, and united with the heart of the King of apostles. Her life as an apostle looked different from the twelve apostles. She entered a cloistered monastery near her home and died of tuberculosis at the age of 24. Yet she was truly an apostle through her prayer and through her love.

She is known for her "little way." Her "little way" is a way of the heart. She writes, "I have no other means of proving my love for you other than that of strewing [scattering] flowers, that is, not allowing one little sacrifice to escape, not one look, one word, profiting by all the smallest things and doing them through love."[6] It is a way of little daily offerings. At each step, she seeks to unite her heart with the heart of Jesus. In this way, each moment of the day has meaning and grace in Christ. For me—and for any of us—answering the door or the phone is an opportunity to greet a son or daughter of God. Doing dishes and household chores is a way to love God and my family. Offering my heart to his heart can contribute to the salvation of all hearts. Each day I can offer my activities to Christ, no matter how small, as a living prayer. With each action, it's as if I'm saying, "Lord, you have shown your love for me, by offering me your heart. Lord, I want to love you ever more—by offering my heart to your heart for all hearts each day."

In her devotion to the Sacred Heart, St. Thérèse felt united with the apostles. Now, let us turn to the apostles at the Ascension of Jesus. There, he sends them forth to preach the Gospel throughout the world. As we reflect on their call, let's consider how Christ is calling us to live the Gospel more fully in our own lives.

OVERVIEW OF THE DAY FROM IGNATIUS: JESUS ASCENDS

St. Ignatius writes, "After Christ our Lord had manifested himself for forty days to the apostles, giving many proofs and signs and speaking about the kingdom of God, he commanded them to wait in Jerusalem for the Holy Spirit he had promised them . . . looking up to heaven, the angels say to them: 'Men of Galilee, why are you standing there looking up at the sky? This Jesus who has been taken from you into heaven will return in the same way as you have seen him going into heaven'" (*SE*, 312).

Jesus appeared to his disciples for forty days after his resurrection from the dead. We celebrate this event during the Easter season each year. Then at the Ascension, he rises to eternal glory with his Father in heaven. The disciples watch him ascend. Why are they looking up to heaven? Why are we? Jesus ascends, and he is still with us. He has not gone away. His mission has not ended. His mission has moved into a new, unexpected final stage: he works through us. Through us, with us, and in us, his Spirit moves our hearts to touch many hearts. We are his Body, the Church. We are nourished by his Body and Blood, the Eucharist. He strengthens us to reach all hearts in a needy and wounded world. This has been his plan all along, however audacious and unthinkable it may seem. He'll save the world through us, one heart at a time.

As my heart is stirred with renewed faith and hope and love, each day I join Jesus in his great mission.

CONTEMPLATION: PENTECOST

After the Ascension of Jesus, the disciples gathered in the upper room and "devoted themselves with one accord to prayer, together with some women, and Mary the mother of Jesus." Nine days after the Ascension, "suddenly there came from the sky a noise like a strong driving wind, and it filled the entire house in which they were. Then there appeared to them tongues as of fire, which parted and came to rest on each one of them. And they were all filled with the holy Spirit" (Acts 1:13–14, 2:2–4).

Let us again use our imaginations to enter into this holy moment with the disciples and Mother Mary. Days earlier, they saw Jesus ascend. This experience brought them joy and confusion. They saw him glorified and united with his Father. Likely they were also filled with questions—the same questions we ask at the end of our retreat: "What is he doing? What now? What happens next?"

They return to prayer in the upper room. This has been the epicenter of the Christian community for the last six weeks. Jesus gathered them in the upper room to share the Eucharist for the first time. After his death on the cross, he appeared there in the Resurrection to the disciples. He returned to the upper room to appear to Thomas, telling him, "Bring your hand and put it into my side, and do not be unbelieving, but believe" (Jn 20:27). We could even say that he brought the upper room to his disciples on the road to Emmaus. "Then they said to each other, 'Were not our hearts burning [within us] while he spoke to us on the way?' . . . Then the two recounted what had taken place on the way and how he was made known to them in the breaking of the bread" (Lk 24:32, 35).

Perhaps there was another, special support to those early disciples in the upper room: Mary's heart. She has a mother's heart, a woman's heart, an immaculate heart. She was the first to feel her son's heartbeat in her womb, and she was the first to lay a hand on the chest of Jesus and feel his tiny heartbeat after his birth. Now she talks with them and prays with them in the upper room. Perhaps Mary's heart offered a quiet, powerful

encouragement to those disciples as she helped to form them
as apostles of prayer after the Ascension. Sometimes she just
listens to them; sometimes she reminds them of Jesus's promis-
es, his words, his miracles, his call, and his friendship. As Mary
followed her son during his preaching and healing, "Mary kept
all these things, reflecting on them in her heart," pondering their
meaning in prayer and likely speaking with him privately afterward (Lk 2:19). As the prophet Simeon said, "and you yourself a
sword will pierce" as she saw her son tortured and killed before
her eyes (Lk 2:35). She did not suffer violence from the soldier's
swords, but in her depth of compassion she suffered internally
with her son. Her heart. She remembers, waits, prays, listens,
and speaks. She knows his mission is not yet complete, even if
she is not certain how he will complete it.

We see two themes in the Resurrection passages: the Sacred
Heart and the Eucharist. An encounter with his heart sets their
hearts on fire. Witnessing his presence in the Eucharist fills their
hearts with hope and joy. Our questions, doubts, and confusion
are transformed into faith and zeal. What next? What more can
he do through us?

The apostles do not have a playbook for life after Pentecost.
They could not skip ahead and read the next chapter in the Acts
of the Apostles: it hadn't been written yet! What do they do?
They do what Jesus did. Peter is preaching. Peter and John heal
a crippled man. "They devoted themselves to meeting together
in the temple area and to breaking bread . . . with exultation and
sincerity of heart" (Acts 2:46). The reference to "breaking bread"

is not simply a reference to a shared meal. Rather, this is a veiled reference to the Eucharist; the risen Jesus is made known to the disciples in the "breaking of the bread." They pray together, eat together, serve the poor together, and have Mass together. They also suffer, are persecuted, and imprisoned. The deacon Stephen dies for his faith, crying out in his final breath as Jesus did, "Into your hands, I commend my spirit."

Jesus calls us to himself. He calls us as friends, family, and community. We pray together, eat together, and celebrate Mass together. We, too, suffer from illness, anxiety, and even persecution. We may not have a playbook for what happens next in our lives. We do know that Jesus wants to walk with us and draw us closer to himself and to one another. He wants to unite my heart with his heart for the salvation of all hearts.

Questions and Exercises

1. Using the tools of Ignatian contemplation (see day 4 to review!), imagine yourself at the scene of Pentecost. Is there anything you want to say to Mary or an apostle? Anything they want to say to you?

2. What is one grace that you have received from this retreat?

3. Is there one additional grace that you need from the Lord? Courage, trust, love?

4. Ask the Lord, "How are you calling me today?" Perhaps to a new mission, a renewed mission, or a deeper engagement with your mission?

SUSCIPE OF ST. IGNATIUS

(*Suscipe* is a Latin word that means "offer." It is pronounced
SOO-shə-pay.)

Take, Lord, and receive all my liberty,
my memory, my understanding,
and my entire will,
All I have and call my own.
You have given all to me.
To you, Lord, I return it.
Everything is yours; do with it what you will.
Give me only your love and your grace,
that is enough for me.

—Spiritual Exercises, 234

CONCLUSION

THE SACRED HEART BEAT: CALL, SEND, REPEAT

Were not our hearts burning within us
while he spoke to us on the way?
—Luke 24:32

This book has invited you to "love him ever more." I hope I have provided a pathway that "draws our heart to be nearer to the Heart of Jesus, to align our hearts with His heart's sentiments, desires and yearnings. It invites us to unite ourselves to the mission which Jesus received from the Father."[1] We travel on this way with Jesus and his friends—that is, the disciples and saints (big and small, official and unofficial). With him, first we explore "my heart," to become more aware of God's blessings and gifts as well as our own wounds and sins. He then shows us "his heart": in the Incarnation, in his call to discipleship, and in his friendship with us. Finally, with him we're sent to touch "all hearts." This mission is rooted in the Church. It begins in our own families, neighborhoods, and parishes. With him, it extends to every heart to the ends of the earth. This is the great mission of compassion to address the needs of the Church and the world.

What happens after that? Well, we pray to reach our final destination: heaven. Christ desires all people to be united with him in love for all eternity. At the end of our retreat, let's reflect on a final image: the heartbeat.

Put your hand over your heart. Feel your heartbeat. Notice the steady rhythm. What is in your heart? Joy and peace? Sorrow and anxiety? All the above? Our hearts are images of God's love for us. Slowly, powerfully, he shares life and grace with us all day every day. Our hearts are also images of the Sacred Heart. Jesus has a living, beating heart right now. His heart is fully human and fully divine. He handcrafted our hearts in the image and likeness of his heart from the first moments of our existence. He continues to shape and bless our hearts through the sacraments, prayer, and his love and grace. His heart still bears the wounds of his public ministry, even pierced by the soldier's lance on the cross. Yet his heart is not simply wounded, but glorified. We ask to unite our wounded hearts to his so that we may also share in his glory.

Our hearts beat. With every beat there is a drawing and sending. Our hearts draw our blood past our lungs, where the blood is refreshed and renewed with every breath of fresh air. Our hearts then send out this new blood into our fingers and toes, elbows and knees, eyes and ears and smile. So, too, with his Sacred Heart. He draws us to himself and sends us out again. He draws us to himself at every Mass, nourishing us with his Body and Blood and sending us out on mission again: "Go forth, the Mass is ended."

If you are feeling exhausted and confused, perhaps this is an invitation to draw closer to his Sacred Heart. We do this in prayer, conversation with faithful friends, on retreat, and in the sacraments. If you are feeling restless and anxious, he may be preparing your heart for a new mission. We need to be drawn and sent every day. Each day should be marked with this rhythm of prayer and service, rest and action, *ora et labora*.

FINAL CONTEMPLATION: "LORD, TOUCH MY HEART"

Let us return to the upper room. There we see the rhythm of drawing and sending. In his resurrection, the risen Jesus gives us his grace. Risen from the dead in body and spirit, he breathes on us and says, "Peace be with you. As the Father has sent me, so I send you" (Jn 20:21). Thomas is not there. Upon his return, Thomas protests, "Unless I see the mark of the nails in his hands . . . I will not believe" (Jn 20:25).

Maybe we feel like we aren't there, either. We each wonder, "Lord, have I encountered your risen body? I feel like I've only seen you suffering. I've experienced my own wounds and failings but have not met you in your glory." A week later Jesus returns and says to Thomas and to us, "'Put your finger here and see my hands, and bring your hand and put it into my side, and do not be unbelieving, but believe.' Thomas answered and said to him, 'My Lord and my God!'" (Jn 20:27–28).

Look at Thomas's heart. He feels frustrated, confused, exhausted. Maybe we do, too. Others claim to experience something that he has not. Jesus hears his prayer and comes to him.

Hear these words of Jesus spoken to us: "Bring your hand and put it into my side." He invites us to reach out and touch his heart. This is the powerful drumbeat at the center of the universe, the infinite love of the eternal God in the heart of his risen Son. Feel his strength, his power, the fire of his love and his tender mercy in the beat of his Sacred Heart. Touch the wound from the soldier's lance.

Now, if we dare, let's continue this contemplation: "Lord, touch my heart." This requires boldness, trust, and openness. Our hearts are wounded, too—by our own sins and those of the world around us. We may feel embarrassed as we see our own hearts. We may feel tempted to turn away. He speaks again: "Courage, daughter!" (Mt 9:22) and "Take courage, it is I, do not be afraid" (Mk 6:50). At our invitation, he reaches out his hand, still bearing the mark of the nail in his palm. His touch reaches our wounds. More deeply, he renews the true image imprinted on our hearts, as beloved sons and daughters of the Father. His touch can transform our wounds, give us strength, and unite our hearts with his. Looking into our eyes, he says, "Peace be with you. As the Father has sent me, so I send you." My heart united with his heart can embrace all hearts in prayer, service, and love.

"Go forth": Jesus sends us. "Do this in memory of me." We don't go alone. We go together as his apostles in prayer. In a grand global community, we are his Body, centered in his heart. Jesus walks with us on this pathway of the heart. We do not walk alone. In the thunder of his heart, our own hearts add their own little rhythms to the song. Our hearts abide in his heart. With him, in a world full of wounded, needy, and broken hearts, we can touch many hearts—yes, all hearts. In the words of St. Ignatius, we do all of this in Christ: AMDG, *Ad Majorem Dei Gloriam*, for the greater glory of God. And as the disciples said to each other, "Were not our hearts burning within us when he spoke to us on the way?" (Lk 24:32).

FINAL HEART CHECK

Take time to review your whole retreat. By reviewing, the Holy Spirit deepens and strengthens the graces you received. Read the questions below. Then take some time for prayer and jot down a few final notes. You could do this now, tomorrow, or over several days next week.

1. How was your retreat? Any surprises?

2. Look over the notes you wrote in your journal during this retreat. What are a few of the highlights/graces? Summarize on a single page.

3. Go back to one of the highlights/graces from your retreat. Review your notes and reflections. Ask the Lord to deepen this grace in your heart. Savor!

4. What is one practice from this retreat that you want to continue in the days ahead?

5. Is there one highlight from this retreat that you want to share with someone in your life? Do it!

APPENDIX

There are many ways to honor the Sacred Heart of Jesus:

- Attend Mass on the first Friday of each month or dedicate special time for prayers that day.
- Pray the Daily Offering (day 7) and include the monthly intention of the pope.
- Enthrone the Sacred Heart of Jesus in your home.[1]
- Consecrate your heart to the heart of Jesus. [2]
- Pray the Litany to the Sacred Heart and John Paul II's Prayer of Consecration to the Sacred Heart.

LITANY OF THE SACRED HEART

(This litany offers thirty-three acclamations to the heart of Jesus in honor of his thirty-three years on earth.)[3]

Lord, have mercy on us. Christ, have mercy on us. Lord, have mercy on us.

Christ, hear us. Christ graciously hear us.

Have mercy on us.

God the Father of Heaven,
God the Son, Redeemer of the world,
God the Holy Spirit,
Holy Trinity, One God,

Heart of Jesus, Son of the Eternal Father,
Heart of Jesus, formed in the womb of the Virgin Mother
    by the Holy Spirit,
Heart of Jesus, united substantially with the word of
    God,
Heart of Jesus, of infinite majesty,
Heart of Jesus, holy temple of God,
Heart of Jesus, tabernacle of the Most High,
Heart of Jesus, house of God and gate of heaven,
Heart of Jesus, glowing furnace of charity,
Heart of Jesus, vessel of justice and love,
Heart of Jesus, full of goodness and love,
Heart of Jesus, abyss of all virtues,
Heart of Jesus, most worthy of all praise,
Heart of Jesus, king and center of all hearts,
Heart of Jesus, in whom are all the treasures of wisdom
    and knowledge,
Heart of Jesus, in whom dwells all the fullness of the
    Divinity,
Heart of Jesus, in whom the Father is well pleased,
Heart of Jesus, from whose fullness we have all received,
Heart of Jesus, desire of the everlasting hills,
Heart of Jesus, patient and rich in mercy,

Heart of Jesus, rich to all who invoke Thee,
Heart of Jesus, fount of life and holiness,
Heart of Jesus, propitiation for our sins,
Heart of Jesus, saturated with revilings,
Heart of Jesus, crushed for our iniquities,
Heart of Jesus, made obedient unto death,
Heart of Jesus, pierced with a lance,
Heart of Jesus, source of all consolation,
Heart of Jesus, our life and resurrection,
Heart of Jesus, our peace and reconciliation,
Heart of Jesus, victim for our sins,
Heart of Jesus, salvation of those who hope in Thee,
Heart of Jesus, hope of those who die in Thee,
Heart of Jesus, delight of all saints,

Lamb of God, who takes away the sins of the world,
    Spare us, oh Lord.
Lamb of God, who takes away the sins of the world,
    Christ graciously spare us.
Lamb of God who takes away the sins of the world,
    Have mercy on us.

Jesus, meek and humble of Heart,
Make our hearts like unto Thine.

Let us pray:
Almighty and everlasting God, look upon the Heart of
    Thy well-beloved Son and upon the acts of praise

and satisfaction which He renders unto Thee in the name of sinners; and do Thou, in Thy great goodness, grant pardon to them who seek Thy mercy, in the name of the same Thy Son, Jesus Christ, who lives and reigns with Thee, world without end. Amen.

JOHN PAUL II'S PRAYER OF CONSECRATION TO THE SACRED HEART

Lord Jesus Christ,
Redeemer of the human race,
to your most Sacred Heart
we turn with humility and trust,
with reverence and hope,
with a deep desire to give to you
glory and honor and praise.

Lord Jesus Christ,
Savior of the world,
we thank you for all that you are
and all that you do for the little flock.

Lord Jesus Christ,
Son of the Living God,
we praise you for the love
that you have revealed
through your Sacred Heart,

which was pierced for us
and which has become the fountain
of our joy, the source of our eternal life.

Gathered together in your Name,
which is above all other names,
we consecrate ourselves to your most Sacred Heart,
in which dwells the fullness of truth and charity.

Lord Jesus Christ,
King of love and Prince of peace,
reign in our hearts and in our homes.
Conquer all the powers of evil
and bring us to share in the victory of your Sacred Heart.
May all we say and do give glory
and praise to you and to the Father
and the Holy Spirit,
one God living
and reigning for ever and ever. Amen.[4]

ANIMA CHRISTI

Soul of Christ, sanctify me
Body of Christ, save me
Blood of Christ, inebriate me
Water from the side of Christ, wash me
Passion of Christ, strengthen me
O good Jesus, hear me

Within Thy wounds hide me
Permit me not to be separated from Thee
From the wicked foe defend me
In the hour of my death call me
And bid me come to Thee
That with Thy angels and saints
I may praise Thee
Forever and ever. Amen.

CENTER OF OUR HEARTS

O God, what will you do to conquer
the fearful hardness of our hearts?
Lord, you must give us new hearts,
to replace hearts that are made of marble and of bronze.
You must give us your own Heart, Jesus.
Come, lovable Heart of Jesus.
Place your Heart deep in the center of our hearts
and enkindle in each heart a flame of love
as strong, as great, as the sum of all the reasons
that I have for loving You, my God.
O holy Heart of Jesus, dwell in my heart,
So that I may live only in you and for you,
So that, in the end, I may live with you eternally in Heaven. Amen.
     —St. Claude de La Colombière, SJ (1641–1682,
          known as the Apostle of the Sacred Heart)[5]

MY CREATOR AT MY CREATION

Lord, you have searched me and you know me:
you know when I sit and stand;
you understand my thoughts from afar.
You created the moon and the stars,
And in great love you made me in your image and
    likeness.
From the first moments of my life,
As you formed me in my mother's womb,
You shaped my very face
Before my mother could kiss my face.
I praise you, because I am wonderfully made;
Know me, God, and know my heart.

—adapted from Psalm 139

PRAYER TO CHRIST THE KING

Eternal Lord of all things,
I make my offering with your favor and help,
I make it in the presence of your infinite goodness,
And of your glorious Mother
and of all the holy men and women
in your heavenly court
I wish and desire, and it is my deliberate decision,
provided only that it for your greater service and praise,
is to imitate you in bearing all injuries and affronts
and any poverty, actual as well as spiritual,

if your Most Holy Divine Majesty desires
to choose and receive me into such a life and state."
                                   —*Spiritual Exercises*, 98

PRAYER FOR GENEROSITY

Lord Jesus, teach me to be generous;
teach me to serve you as you deserve,
to give and not to count the cost,
to fight and not to heed the wounds,
to toil and not to seek for rest,
to labor and not to seek reward,
except that of knowing that I do your will.
                                   —traditional Jesuit prayer

PRAYER OF ST. FRANCIS

Make me a channel of your peace
Where there is hatred let me bring your love
Where there is injury, your pardon Lord
And where there is doubt true faith in You
Make me a channel of your peace
Where there is despair in life let me bring hope
Where there is darkness only light
And where there's sadness ever joy
Oh, Master, grant that I may never seek
So much to be consoled as to console
To be understood as to understand

To be loved as to love with all my soul
Make me a channel of your peace
It is in pardoning that we are pardoned
It is in giving to all that we receive
And in dying that we are born to eternal life.

PRAYER TO LOVE GOD WITH ALL MY HEART

My God, I love thee;
not because I hope for heaven,
nor because I fear the fires of hell.
Thou, O my Jesus,
did embrace me upon the cross;
and did bear for me the nails and spear,
and manifold disgrace.
And griefs and torments and sweat of agony;
even death itself,
and all for me, a sinner indeed.
Then why, O blessed Jesus Christ
should I not love thee well?
not for the hope of winning heaven,
or of escaping hell.
not with the hope of gain,
nor seeking a reward,
but as thyself has loved me,
O ever-loving Lord!
Even so I love thee, and will love thee
and thy praise I will sing,

solely because thou art my God,
and my eternal king.

—St. Francis Xavier, SJ[6]

PRAYER TO THE CHRIST CHILD

O Little Infant Jesus, my only treasure,
I abandon myself to Your every wish.
I seek no other joy than that of calling forth Your sweet
    smile.
Grant me the graces and the virtues of Your Holy
    Childhood,
so that on the day of my birth into Heaven
the angels and saints may recognize me as truly Yours.

—St. Thérèse of Lisieux[7]

SUSCIPE OF ST. IGNATIUS

Take, Lord, and receive all my liberty,
my memory, my understanding,
and my entire will,
All I have and call my own.
You have given all to me.
To you, Lord, I return it.
Everything is yours; do with it what you will.
Give me only your love and your grace,
that is enough for me.

—*Spiritual Exercises*, 234

NOTES

ACKNOWLEDGMENTS

1. The Way of the Heart was developed in 2017 by Fr. Frederic Fornos, SJ, international director of Pope's Worldwide Prayer Network (PWPN). Visit popesprayer.va/way-of-the-heart/ and caminodelcorazon.church/web/ (at publication, only in Spanish) for more information.

INTRODUCTION

1. All excerpts from St. Ignatius's *Spiritual Exercises* (*SE*) are from the translation by George E. Ganss, SJ, Chestnut Hill, MA: Institute of Jesuit Sources, 1992. Used with permission from the Institute for Advanced Jesuit Studies. (Excerpts are cited with the paragraph number, which is consistent across editions and translations.)

DAY 2

1. Ignatius Loyola, *Autobiography*, para. 5, in *St. Ignatius of Loyola, Personal Writings* (Penguin Books, London: 2004).

2. The book on the saints was *The Golden Legend*, a heroic retelling of the saints' lives and exploits. The other book was Ludolf of Saxony's *The Life of Christ*, a devotional book that helps the reader to imagine gospel scenes and to dialogue with Jesus in prayer.

3. Ignatius Loyola, *Autobiography*, para. 7.

4. Ignatius Loyola, *Autobiography*, para. 8.

DAY 3

1. This section is adapted from author's essay, "A Deadly Crash on the Feast of the Assumption," *America*, August 2019, americamagazine.org/faith/2019/08/15/deadly-crash-feast-assumption.

2. Francis, "Homily for the Opening of the XIV Ordinary General Assembly of the Synod of Bishops (Rome, October 4, 2015), vatican.va/content/francesco/en/homilies/2015/documents/papa-francesco_20151004_omelia-apertura-sinodo-vescovi.html.

3. Thomas Aquinas, *Summa Theologica* 2.2, Q. 162, A. 1."There is a good and an evil pride"; or "a sinful pride which God resists, and a pride that denotes the glory which He bestows;" newadvent.org/summa/3162.htm.

4. Thomas Aquinas, *Summa contra Gentiles*, bk. 4, chap. 55, in Arthur Devine, "Humility," *The Catholic Encyclopedia*, vol. 7 (New York: Robert Appleton Company, 1910), newadvent.org/cathen/07543b.htm.

5. "Prayer of St. Francis Xavier," www.liturgies.net, accessed March 11, 2022, liturgies.net/saints/francisxavier/prayers.htm.

DAY 4

1. Adapted into contemporary language by the author from "Prayers of St. Thérèse," Our Catholic Prayers, accessed March 11, 2022, ourcatholicprayers.com/prayers-of-st-therese.html.

DAY 6

1. *The Autobiography of St. Margaret Mary Alacoque* (Charlotte, NC: Tan Books, 2012), sec. 83.

2. I am compressing several months and experiences from the life of St. Margaret Mary to imaginatively (and faithfully) sketch out her surroundings and visions. See her autobiography and letters for more information, cited above and below.

3. *Letters of St. Margaret Mary Alacoque*, translated by Fr. Clarence Herbst, SJ (Charlotte, NC: Tan Books, 1997), Letter 133; see also *Autobiography of St. Margaret Mary Alacoque*, sec. 53.

4. Adapted from *St. Margaret Mary Alacoque,* Letter 132. Herbst uses the word "abyss;" I have opted for "ocean," as I think this better captures her meaning.

5. *The Spiritual Direction of St. Claude de la Colombiere,* translated by Mother M. Phillip (San Francisco: Ignatius Press, 2018), 46.

6. I am indebted to Fr. David Stanley, SJ, for this reflection. He wrote a famous essay on "Took, Blessed, Broke and Gave," in his book *A Modern Scriptural Approach to the "Spiritual Exercises"* (Institute of Jesuit Sources, St. Louis, 1967). I have used his structure but applied it in a new way for this chapter.

7. The Anima Christi was a favorite prayer of St. Ignatius and dates to the early 1400s.

DAY 7

1. Homily for the feast of St. Francis Xavier, accessed March 13, 2022, https://popesprayerusa.net/history/.

2. This is an imagined scene, based on letters and descriptions from this period. It condenses several weeks and conversations. I hope it captures some of the drama and grace of the beginnings of the Apostleship of Prayer.

3. Office of Readings, St. John Brébeuf, Feast of North American Martyrs.

4. Office of Readings, Feast of St. Francis Xavier.

5. *Sergio Palagiano,* "Exploring the Apostleship of Prayer Collection at the Archivum Romanum Societatis Iesu (ARSI): Between Archival Analysis and Research Perspectives," Portal to Jesuit Studies, March 1, 2021, jesuitportal.bc.edu/publications/symposia/2019symposium/symposia-palagiano/.

6. "History," Pope's Worldwide Prayer Network, accessed March 13, 2022, popesprayerusa.net/history/.

7. "History," Pope's Worldwide Prayer Network; see also R. P. Ramière, *Manual of the Apostleship of Prayer*

(Dublin: John F. Fowler, 1864), google.com/books/edition/Manual_of_the_Apostleship_of_Prayer.

8. "The Jesuits and the Devotion to the Heart of Jesus," accessed March 13, 2022, popesprayer.va/wp-content/uploads/2021/05/1-The-Jesuits-and-Devotion-to-the-Heart-of-Jesus-ENG-DEF.pdf.

9. The Holy Father's prayer intentions for each month can be found at http://popesprayerusa.net/popes-intentions/.

10. Pope Francis, General Audience, St. Peter's Square, Rome, March 27, 2013, vatican.va/content/francesco/en/audiences/2013/documents/papa-francesco_20130327_udienza-generale.html.

11. Michael Harter, *Hearts on Fire: Praying with Jesuits* (St. Louis, MO: Institute of Jesuit Sources, 1993), 54.

DAY 8

1. This prayer is inspired by the life of St. Francis of Assisi and has been set to music by various artists. It was first published in 1912 in French, in the Catholic magazine *La Clochette*.

DAY 9

1. Courtney Mares, "'The Heart of the Church's Mission Is Prayer,' Pope Francis Says," Catholic News Agency, June 28, 2019, catholicnewsagency.com/news/41670/the-heart-of-the-churchs-mission-is-prayer-pope-francis-says.

2. Francis, Lenten message, sec. 3, Libreria Editrice Vaticana, 2015, https://www.vatican.va/content/francesco/en/messages/lent/documents/papa-francesco_20141004_messaggio-quaresima2015.html.

3. Thérèse Martin's membership card can be viewed online, accessed March 13, 2022, http://popesprayerusa.net/2018/10/01/young-heart-open-world-saint-therese-lisieux/.

4. *The Autobiography of St. Thérèse of Lisieux: The Story of a Soul*, trans. John Clarke, OCD (Washington, DC: ICS Publications, 1996), ch. 9. Emphases in original.

5. *The Autobiography of St. Thérèse of Lisieux*, ch. 9.

6. *The Autobiography of St. Thérèse of Lisieux*, ch. 9.

CONCLUSION

1. "The Way of the Heart," Pope's Worldwide Prayer Network, accessed March 13, 2022, popesprayer.va/way-of-the-heart/.

APPENDIX

1. The Sacred Heart Enthronement Network provides detailed instructions at welcomehisheart.com.

2. "Act of Consecration to the Sacred Heart," EWTN, accessed March 13, 2022, https://www.ewtn.com/catholicism/devotions/act-of-consecration-to-the-sacred-heart-12727.

3. "The Litany of the Sacred Heart of Jesus," EWTN, accessed March 13, 2022, ewtn.com/catholicism/devotions/litany-of-the-sacred-heart-of-jesus-12754.

4. Adapted from "Prayer of John Paul II on Occasion of the Visit to the Cathedral of the Sacred Heart," Delhi, India, February 1, 1986, vatican.va/content/john-paul-ii/en/speeches/1986/february/documents/hf_jp-ii_spe_19860201_preghiera-cattedrale-delhi.html.

5. Harter, *Hearts on Fire*, 54.

6. "Prayer of St. Francis Xavier," www.liturgies.net, accessed March 11, 2022, liturgies.net/saints/francisxavier/prayers.htm.

7. Adapted into contemporary language by the author from "Prayers of St. Thérèse," Our Catholic Prayers, accessed March 11, 2022, ourcatholicprayers.com/prayers-of-st-therese.html.

FR. JOE LARAMIE, SJ, is national director of the Pope's Worldwide Prayer Network (Apostleship of Prayer) and the author of *Abide in the Heart of Christ*. He previously served as a campus minister at St. Louis University, where he earned his undergraduate and master's degrees in communications. He studied at Kenrick-Glennon Seminary prior to joining the Jesuit novitiate. Laramie earned master of divinity and licentiate degrees in theology at Boston College. He was ordained a priest in 2011.

Laramie's ministry has included working with the homeless in Minnesota and Oregon and with hospital patients in Chicago, Illinois. He taught at Regis Jesuit High School in Aurora, Colorado, and Rockhurst High School in Kansas City, Missouri, and also worked as a missionary to Mayan villages in Belize. Laramie served as a preacher and spiritual director at White House Jesuit Retreat house in St. Louis, Missouri. Laramie's work has appeared in *America* magazine, the Hallow app, and *Ave Spotlight*. He has been a guest on *Busted Halo*, EWTN radio and TV, the *Jesuitical* podcast, and Leah Darrow's *Lux U.*

joelaramiesj.com
popesprayerusa.net

Facebook: Joe Laramie SJ, Pope's Worldwide Prayer Network USA
Instagram: @JoeLaramieSJ, @popesprayerusa
Twitter: @JoeLaramieSJ, @popesprayerusa

ALSO BY
JOE LARAMIE, SJ

Abide in the Heart of Christ
A 10-Day Personal Retreat with St. Ignatius Loyola

Books and spiritual leaders often mention the importance of growing closer to Christ, but this can seem impossible without a guide. *Abide in the Heart of Christ* by Fr. Joe Laramie, SJ, acts as that teacher, offering readers wisdom from the foundations of Ignatian spirituality in an accessible, ten-day format. This retreat in daily life helps readers to encounter Christ, grow in relationship with him, and shape their hearts according to his desire.
